i nam
my dog
pushkin

**(and other
immigrant tales)**

i named my dog pushkin

(and other immigrant tales)

notes from
a soviet girl
on becoming
an american
woman

**margarita
gokun silver**

Thread

Published by Thread in 2021

An imprint of Storyfire Ltd.
Carmelite House
50 Victoria Embankment
London EC4Y 0DZ

www.thread-books.com

ISBN: 978-1-90977-066-9
eBook ISBN: 978-1-80019-534-9

Printed and bound in Great Britain

The FSC® label means that materials used for the product
have been responsibly sourced.

To my thesaurus.

TABLE OF CONTENTS

THE PREFACE

(a.k.a. facts that may or may not be useful as you read this collection.)

1) I cannot swear in my native language because decency exists, but I swear in English as if I was born to do it. I hope you enjoy.

2) Applying the definition "first generation American" equally to your parents, you, and your child born in the US is like saying there's no difference between *pelmeni*, ravioli, dumplings, and *vareniki* because flour is one of the ingredients.

3) When Russians talk to each other in Russian, they are not fighting.

4) You don't speak the same language as your immigrant parents when you explain things to them, no matter what anyone's told you.

5) If you think your immigrant parents' opinion of your immigration journey doesn't really affect you 30+ years after you immigrated, you are wrong.

6) The Russian accent in English absolutely sounds villainous, Trevor Noah was 100 percent right about that.

7) Putin's first name in Russian means "to own the world" and that is his exact aspiration. Be careful what you wish for when you name your child.

THE GLOSSARY

Babushka: A grandmother. Alternatively, an older lady working as a guard in a museum, a keys custodian in a hospital, or a warden in a Palace of Young Pioneers. Basically, a Soviet bouncer who completely lacks the bouncer physique but more than makes up for it in attitude.

Babushkas: Plural for grandmother. Also, a group of older ladies who, seemingly 24/7, sat on strategically-positioned-for-gossip neighborhood benches. With spying power possibly unrivaled by any world-class security agency, they blathered about everything from the loose morals of teenage girls to the terrible parenting of mothers who didn't put hats on their babies when the temperatures dipped below 20 °C. Honestly, I don't understand how the KGB didn't think of tapping into this resource when spying on us. Or maybe they did. Maybe we just didn't know.

Blat: Known as "your network of useful connections with high-level Communist Party *apparatchiks*, warehouse directors, theater administrators, store, restaurant, hotel, and sanatorium managers, and other valuable people with access to goods and services never available out in the open in our communism-bound land of plenty" and known in my family as "*babushka* Olga," my paternal grandmother.

Dedushka: A grandfather. In this collection, always *my* grandfather.

Fifth line: Not to be confused with the "fifth column" but potentially thought of as such by the Soviet establishment. A line in any Soviet citizen's passport that delineated their *natsional'nost'* (ethnic origin). Used by Jews as a metaphor to describe institutionalized antisemitism because it was a handy, concise explanation of why you weren't as good as everyone else.

Zhidovka: The female version of an offensive Russian slur for a Jewish person (*zhid* for a male). Also known as a term of endearment if you were a Jewish teenage girl and he was a Russian teenage boy. Think of it as the equivalent of an infatuated boy pulling on a girl's braid—except that in this situation the girl has no braids and is Jewish.

Why Pushkin? Is this book about a dog? Who is the real Pushkin and why is naming a dog after him a big deal (is it?)? WHAT IS THIS BOOK ABOUT? I DON'T UNDERSTAND IT!

All of these questions—and more—are answered in The Introduction.

THE INTRODUCTION

Amerika was evil (according to the Politburo).

Amerika was forbidden (also according to the Politburo).

Amerika had Levi's (according to an occasional sighting of a JC Penney catalogue passed around our school with as much reverence as if it were the Levi's themselves).

Those three (but especially the last) were enough for almost every Soviet teenager to love *Amerika*. There wasn't a student at my school and, later, at my university who didn't fantasize about moving to the United States—or *Amerika* as we called it—about picking up dollars off the streets, about buying the boat-sized Buick we'd seen in pirated *Miami Vice* episodes with those dollars, and about parading their collection of Levi's in New York City (the only city worth parading them in, though also we didn't really know of too many other cities in *Amerika*).

But they only fantasized about it. I was about to do it.

The year was 1989. I was a 20-year-old engineering student at the Moscow Institute of Oil and Gas and I'd just gleefully finished informing the dean that they wouldn't see me in lectures in the fall. Gleefully because I was dropping out to emigrate to *Amerika* (and also because this meant I wouldn't have to sit for a gas storage facilities final).

"Won't you miss it?" he asked me. "Miss your *Rodina*, your Motherland?"

15

A Soviet bureaucrat with a receding hairline, a crumpled suit, and at least a 30-year membership in the Communist Party, he definitely wasn't someone I'd choose for a heart-to-heart conversation. Especially not about my growing ambivalence towards the Soviet Union and the idea it was actually good enough to be a Motherland (also towards thermodynamics lectures). No, I wasn't going to miss it, but he didn't need to know that.

"Of course, I will," I said.

"So why are you leaving?"

"My parents," I lied. "They're making me."

I lied because it was the other way around. Two years earlier—and for almost 12 consecutive months—I'd hounded my mother and father to agree to a move I'd presented as our ticket to "everything better." For them, and for my grandparents, this "everything" included possibly better living conditions, potentially better work opportunities, and definitely better health care. For me, it basically came down to just one thing—a better chance of escape. I knew that if I ever planned to get those Levi's, and maybe have a taste of what Bruce Springsteen sang about (those who claimed to understand English told us it was sex and freedom but mainly freedom), I had to run. Run from both the tight yoke and the antisemitic merry-go-round of the Soviet system, and from the suffocating control of my parents. Because—just like any respectable Soviet progenitors—they believed they were in charge of me and my life.

When that Aeroflot plane took off on October 19, 1989 from the Moscow Sheremetyevo airport with me and my parents on board, I had only one important objective—to stop being Russian.[1] Technically, we had already achieved that because, when we decided to emigrate, the Soviet Union basically wrote us out of its life, and by that I mean they revoked our citizenship while calling us "rats fleeing the sinking ship." But my aim was to become a *fully fledged* American and I knew that simply losing your red Soviet passport wasn't going to cut it.

Here's what was going to cut it:

- Buying a pair of Levi's immediately on landing.
- Not befriending, not dating, and not marrying any of my former compatriots *ever.*
- Correcting everyone who'd ask, "Oh, you're Russian?" with, "No, I'm from Russia" (or the Soviet Union, depending on the time frame obviously).
- Never confusing "skirt" and "shirt," making sure I didn't say "wind" when I meant "wind" [waɪnd], and working on the pronunciation of the words "sheet" and "beach."
- Training my face *not* to look Russian, which basically meant eliminating that hardened, cynical, don't-you-jump-in-front-of-me-in-line expression so many of us had perfected.
- Losing my villainy-sounding Russian accent when speaking English.

---

1 I had another important objective and that was *not* to crash, but since this was outside my control and in the hands of an airline that seemed to crash their planes every other day, I can't really claim it as *my* objective.

I had several reasons for wanting to disavow every bit of Russian heritage, but the most important one was that *I didn't have one.* That, at least, was according to the highest echelons of the Soviet bureaucracy, the Constitution, and also the guy two floors down who regularly pointed out to me that Russia wasn't for Jews.

Jewish citizens of the USSR were not Russian, would never be allowed to be Russian, and would be laughed at if they showed up at a passport office and asked to be recorded as Russian. The fifth line of every Soviet passport was there to keep you in the place in which you belonged and therefore if you were a Jew, you were written up as a Jew, if you were Ukrainian you were written up as Ukrainian, if you were Armenian, you were written up as Armenian, if you were… you get the gist. Your *natsional'nost*[2] was yours for life and came complete with colorful bigotry, ingeniously insidious discrimination, and self-worth so low that basically the only way was up.

There was a joke that circulated in the Soviet émigré circles of the early 1990s in the US. "To get a landline," it said, "we had to wait 20 years and one day—20 years in the Soviet Union and one day in the US." I'm going to go ahead and apply the same joke to becoming Russian. This elusive designation that all of us were so desperate for and could never get while living in the USSR was now bestowed on us by every American, no questions asked, no passport examined, no fifth line scrutinized with eyebrows furrowed and lips pursed. Russian who? No, thanks, NOT FOR ME.

---

2 Translated as "ethnic origin" for other nationalities of the USSR, and as "your worst nightmare" for Jews.

Maybe I was too touchy. Or perhaps even a tad dramatic (my mother thinks so). But why would I want to belong to a culture that never wanted me in the first place? Why would I go proudly inflating my chest at mentions of Dostoevsky, Swan Lake, and the high cheekbones and long legs Russian women were famed for the world over (especially because I didn't have *either* of the latter two)? And although mine wasn't a grievance against any of those per se,[3] I felt very strongly that if the country was going to treat me like a failed Olympian with zero chances at a medal, I was going to treat it like an Olympian who defected and then won all the medals. Which basically meant I'd become completely American, disavow anything and everything Russian, and then—after I grew filthy rich and ultra-famous—I'd ignore my former Motherland in the same spectacular fashion it had rejected me. If this sounds petty, that's because it is.

Now, the bad news is that I'm still working on becoming rich and famous. But the good news is that I haven't felt any pride towards anything Russian for years. Which, honestly, hasn't been that hard for reasons you'll learn in these essays, but also because obviously I'm good at holding grudges.[4] So when my daughter declared she wanted a dog and I got her one while living in St. Petersburg, Russia—

---

3 Although, let's be honest, many of the Russian classic writers were rabid antisemites—a fact I had to stoically ignore while writing complimentary essays about them in high school.

4 And also because of Putin and his scheming KGB ass to get vengeance for the break-up of the Soviet Union *by trying to destabilize the US with an army of bots.*

having returned for a job 16 years after I left the country—I gave him the most fitting name an animal who was born there could have. I named him after one of the city's (and the country's) most famous sons.

In retrospect, here are the things I should have known before naming my dog Pushkin:

- It's not a good idea if you're living in Russia.
- It's an even worse idea if you're living in Russia and you're a native Russian speaker.
- It's like waving an American flag on Red Square during one of those Soviet era military parades with nuclear warheads pointing directly at you—if you're living in Russia, you're a native Russian speaker, and you're calling your dog to come to you on the street.

But none of the above occurred to me. Mainly because my Stakhanovite efforts to turn myself from someone born in the Soviet Union into an American had clearly succeeded, but also because naming a dog after a famous Russian poet seemed like a great idea at the time. Really, what better way is there to remember your dog's Russian origins than to be reminded of the rich poetic history of those origins?

But the Russians who heard me scold him for chasing a stray cat, or praise him for doing his business in a bed of flowers disagreed. "You named your dog after our most revered poet?" a *babushka* once asked me. I nodded while Pushkin lifted his leg against the base of the statue of Gogol. "That's awful!" she said, shaking her head. "So disrespectful."

I wanted to point out that it was actually quite respectful because Pushkin was a small, pure-bred Maltese who was both adorable and hypoallergenic. He had hair, not fur, which made him closer to humans than any other dog. Plus, when short, his hair was curly and not at all dissimilar to that of the real Pushkin (if you don't pay attention to the color, which you shouldn't because that's not the point). He was also very quiet and well behaved, and who could tell that in his moments of retrospection he wasn't writing his own special brand of dog poetry? And finally, what better way was there to pay homage to a poet than to call his name several times a day? But as I prepared to delve into these explanations and outline the comparisons I felt benefitted both the poet and the dog, she puffed in disgust and turned away to speak to another *babushka* about my unfitness to be Russian and possibly about turning me in.

From that encounter I learned this:

1) Pushkin was better off peeing and pooping on a pad indoors both because I didn't want to unnerve any *babushka* badly enough to cause a heart attack and because St. Petersburg's winter was as cold as hell that freezes over not once but twice and, unlike the real Pushkin, our dog didn't own a mink coat.

2) If he had to go out, we'd invent endearing nicknames which he'd answer to but which wouldn't betray his connection with a dead poet. That's how *Pusch-wosch, Puschie*, and *Poopster* were born.

3) *Babushkas* seemed just as vicious in twenty-first century Russia as they were in the Soviet Union when I lived there. THANK GOD I LEFT.

This book isn't about a dog (although he's adorable and does deserve a book, especially since his namesake has quite a few). It's also not about Russian literary history, its giants, or the *babushkas* who guard them. And it's definitely not about whether or not naming your dog after one of those literary giants is such a huge faux pas that it could qualify you for the status of the worst emigrant ever.

But this book is about immigration. It's about what it's like for a young woman to leave one country, land in another, and build a new life. It's about that building process which doesn't come with instructions but, instead, includes a lot of people who stare at you when all you want is an extra "shit"[5] of paper. It's about a path that's supposedly yours to discover but also yours to screw up, be criticized for, and feel really guilty about. It's about your voice—the voice you're supposed to find and nurture when everyone keeps interrupting you, or shushing you, or calling you tone deaf. It's about having to scream to be heard, or singing off-tune, or speaking a language no one gets and consequently getting lost and confused and embarrassed, and also ashamed.

Because you're an immigrant and a woman, and being both isn't easy. And because your acts of defiance—naming your dog after Pushkin apparently among them—don't often endear you to others.

But, no, really, it's a funny book.

---

5 Okay, fine, I didn't always stretch that vowel long enough to sound decent.

IMMIGRATION PART 1,
OR RULES, WHAT RULES?

To win at life in the Soviet Union you needed to know four things:

1) A law isn't a law unless you find a way around it.[1]
2) Grow your *blat* at any opportunity.
3) Make sure to offer a bribe whenever possible.[2]
4) That Young Pioneer thing they taught you that "the truth will always come out" and therefore you shouldn't lie? Don't worry about it. Take all the chances you get.

To win at life in our household you needed to know one more thing:

5) Never come back after leaving the house; but if you do, make *absolutely* sure you look in the mirror because if you don't, all kinds of misfortune will befall you.[3]

---

1 In the US, this is called a loophole.

2 In the US, this is called lobbying.

3 My cousin tells me that everyone she knew in Odessa followed this rule, and a few former compatriots tell me that this is actually a Russian superstition, which probably means mirror looking was more widespread than I realized at the time. Maybe that's why hallway mirrors were fairly easy to buy?

My mother claims that on the day of our emigration I forgot that last one, and that's why things didn't go as planned. I disagree because things went perfectly fine after they almost didn't and, anyway, I could distinctly remember looking in the mirror several times, some of them even for longer than a moment, which is the general guideline.

Let me explain.

On the morning of our emigration, when my dad was already downstairs squeezing our suitcases into a taxi and my mother and I were locking up our apartment (which looked like Russia immediately post Ghenghis Khan's thirteenth-century invasion), I remembered that I had forgotten my favorite scarf. Because I had only thought of it as soon as my mother had closed the door and locked up the apartment, my potential going back would break the last rule, thus encouraging all of the bad luck in the immediate (and not so immediate) vicinity to fall on our shoulders. My mother pointed out that I could ruin everything by stepping across that threshold and couldn't I just buy another scarf when we got there? I swore like the good Pioneer I once was that I would look in the mirror and would even do it three times for good measure, at which point she gave up because it was the morning she was leaving her country forever and arguing with me wasn't high on her priority list. I walked back in, found my scarf, looked in the mirror, then did it again, and then again, and was about to walk out when the phone rang. At this point I figured what the hell, this was the last call I'd ever answer in Moscow and what if it was that sport lotto I had played three years ago and they were finally calling to tell me

I'd won a 5,000 roubles jackpot?[4] I sat down on the only uncluttered horizontal space—the vacuum cleaner that doubled as a stool in every cramped Soviet apartment—and picked up the receiver. To my dismay, it wasn't the sport lotto people but a school classmate who'd just returned from his two years in the Red Army and was calling around to see if people wanted to hang out.

"What are you doing tomorrow?" he asked.

I imagined telling him the truth would not be a good idea. Like saying, "Hey, so I know you just spent two years getting hazed and generally being terrified they'd send you on the next train to fight in Afghanistan, but yeah, I'm on my way to capitalist America, see you, bye!" would actually be like rubbing salt on those hazing wounds he probably still nursed.

So instead I said, "I have no idea, but call tomorrow and maybe we'll do something."

"Sure," he said, and we hung up. I stared in the mirror extra hard just to make sure, grabbed my scarf, and left.

In the customs line later that morning I was seized with doubt that the jinxing Gods existed or that they were actually *present* when I did my dutiful mirror staring. Because in front of me, Soviet customs officials were amassing such a loot of confiscated items that it could have financed the second Afghan War and another nuclear warhead to aim at the United States. That was because all of the émigrés in front of us lived by the aforementioned rule #4 (lying makes the world go around despite what your inner Young Pioneer might say) and had

---

4 Around 5 US cents in actual, usable currency but who cares—it was the principle of it.

packed more jewelry than they were allowed.[5] Which I had as well—but I had a very good excuse to be bringing this extra silver bangle that was now jammed so high up my arm that gangrene was imminent.

The bracelet was a gift from my grandmother who had died ten days before we left. She was supposed to come with us—she had a ticket, an exit visa and her very own suitcases—when ten days before our flight she had a stroke. The Soviet medical establishment being what it was didn't manage to save her, and now I was in line trying to smuggle the only memory I had left of her under my jacket sleeve. That's because I was too naive to imagine that Soviet customs had evolved from body cavity searches to shiny new electronic devices that beeped in the proximity of any forbidden heirloom, no invasive procedures necessary.

Very obviously I freaked out and also very obviously my mother elbowed me and mouthed that she had predicted this when she had told me NOT TO GO BACK FOR MY SCARF. What she meant to communicate was that anything could happen now, and that we could get discovered smuggling out a silver bangle, get our exit visas ripped in half, and be escorted under a heavy police presence to the first Siberian camp where they had a vacancy, and it would be all my fault *because I went back for my scarf.*

I wanted to point out that I *did* look in the mirror and that it wasn't my fault if there had been some kind of disconnect in that

5 Each person was allowed two silver or gold items and $80 in hard currency—either because the Politburo believed that a lifetime of work in the Soviet Union couldn't net anyone more than that, or because they just wanted to pocket the rest. Probably the latter.

rule's time-space continuum, but I didn't have the time. A customs officer was waving me over, presumably to arrest me because he didn't even need that beeping traitor since my face was plainly saying, "I have an extra bracelet on my arm, please don't shoot me." But he must not have been very good at face reading, because he stood me next to a table with the loot and also with a whole bunch of kopeks[6] other émigrés had discarded because they weren't valid currency in the West. He passed that devil along my arms and it beeped exactly where it was supposed to, and I melted into the cement floor and they had to scrape me off wearing hazmat suits because obviously a melting human being is something to be concerned about. But it appeared that the jinxing Gods were watching over me because as I was doing my melting, the officer was staring at the pile of kopeks and then at his beeping device and then at the pile of kopeks again, confused into thinking it was beeping *because* of those kopeks.

In the end, he let me through with my bracelet and this was the first time I ever felt respect towards kopeks, because really you couldn't buy anything with them ever except for maybe a box of matches. Also, I had a chance to say "I told you so" to my mom and it felt good, mainly because it was evidence I was a good daughter and had in fact looked into the mirror, but also because I wanted her to know I was right.

---

6 A Soviet penny a.k.a. the pride and joy of our socialist economy because you could buy a box of matches for one kopek and place a phone call from a public phone booth for two. Which capitalist penny could do that in the 1980s?

On landing at the airport in Vienna I mentally put together what people would now call my "vision board." It looked something like this:

GOAL: Be like these people.

By these people, I didn't mean, of course, my fellow émigrés who clutched their scuffed Soviet suitcases, along with the bundles containing grandma's old tea set that didn't fit into those suitcases, and stood gaping as if they'd just woken up in Brezhnev's Crimea Palace. I meant those other passengers—THE WESTERNERS—who were purposefully walking from point A to point B wearing beautiful clothes and glasses that weren't fixed with tape while pulling *wheeled* suitcases around us with enough distance, just in case we still glowed in the dark post-Chernobyl.

With that vision board in mind, I followed my parents and the rest of the immigrant contingent to the exit to start working on that goal and also to catch the van we'd been told would pick us up. There was no van, but a very insistent airport official told us to go and wait around the corner and, because we were recently Soviet and were accustomed to not questioning authorities at the risk of being shot, we dragged our suitcases and bundles the length of the building to stand far away from the arrivals hall where there were no well-dressed people to shock. There were also no benches.

We sat on that curbside for the NEXT FIVE HOURS. Those of us who remembered rule #3 and had bribed Sheremetyevo baggage handlers *not* to cut our suitcases and steal smoked sausages out of them, took those sausages out and shared them with the rest of the group. Because we had no money we couldn't call anyone to inquire about the van, but even if we had money we wouldn't have known who to call. And also, that would have required us to leave our area behind the building and what if that official was still there? At some point, it began to drizzle and some of us wondered if the van was coming at all and what we would do if it didn't come. My father wondered what the hell he—a professional engineer with a degree and many years of experience stapling pipelines in Siberia—was doing on a curbside behind the Vienna airport building. My mother gave me a look which spelled out her disappointment that I had gone back for my scarf, and I didn't appreciate it because I was already sad about my vision board and its goal. How was I ever going to reach it if I wasn't even allowed to be among the people I wanted to become? Then, just as I was about to explain to my mother that I would have been an icicle by now had it not been for that scarf, a white van finally rounded the corner and things began to look up.

But they only looked up until the van dropped us off at what they called a "pension" and what my parents called "a complete disgrace" because we were put up in bunk beds in a large room with several other families. My father immediately went downstairs to complain because he was a professional engineer with a degree and many years of experience of stapling pipelines in Siberia and he hadn't even lived like this when he was a Soviet student. But the clerk downstairs spoke no Russian and we didn't have any money for a bribe. We spent the next three weeks sleeping in bunk beds and finishing what was left of the sausages, which we ate with potatoes and sauerkraut we bought in a local store.

Because Austria was the first Western country we had ever set foot in we spent an inordinate amount of time deciphering capitalism. For example, was a 1,200 schilling price tag expensive for the most beautiful pair of boots you've ever seen? Was the Ramada hotel as exclusive as the Intourist? Why were these people waiting at a crosswalk if there were *no* cars? Was that a rule? How many flea markets would we have to visit before we finally sold that pair of pointe shoes we had brought with us because the émigré rumor mill claimed Russian-made pointe shoes were all the rage in the West? What was a tampon?

By the time we finally found our footing in Austria (and by that I mean we figured out which sauerkraut jar was a better deal), we were shipped to Italy for the second and final leg of our immigration journey. Shipped, because that's pretty much exactly how our transport went:

- We were told to assemble at a train station where we came carrying our suitcases and our bundles and whatever sauerkraut we hadn't finished.
- There we discovered we would travel on a train with *no* bunks. That was shocking for two reasons: (1) it was an overnight train, and (2) aren't people supposed to sleep in a horizontal position at night and what the hell were we supposed to do in compartments that had six seats each and no place to lie down?
- There was no space for our suitcases anywhere in that compartment. We wedged them between the seats, which left no space for our legs, and we spent the entire night unable to sleep while our legs fell asleep just fine and *constantly*.

- Austrian police with machine guns were stationed at the end of each car. Later the Italian Carabinieri replaced them.
- If all of the above doesn't strike you like some kind of Nazi déjà vu, just wait.
- At dawn, we were told we'd have a total of two minutes to disembark at a small station on the outskirts of Rome. This might have been sufficient for an Italian with a wheeled suitcase, but it was *not* sufficient for an émigré with several suitcases, bundles, children, and frail grandparents. On the plus side, those grandparents still remembered World War II and how to evacuate a bombed-out train. Which is what we did, throwing luggage and passing the children through the windows and disregarding the doors.
- If all of the above still doesn't strike you like some kind of Nazi déjà vu, just wait.
- After the train left and the Italians who disembarked ran away fearing that the Russians were coming and no one told them, a man wearing *a black leather coat and tall black leather boots* appeared from nowhere and began to scream at us in Italian.
- I wondered if this was some kind of sick joke or if we were all about to die, because he looked like an actual Nazi from 1941.
- Everyone else wondered the same thing.
- The man screamed louder because no one understood him and it's a known fact that loudness makes people understand foreign languages.
- At this point my mother could think of no better solution than to elbow me and tell me to go and translate for him

because I took Italian before we left Moscow and also because, obviously, she no longer wanted a daughter.

- To which I said, "Nope, absolutely no way, this is not how I want to die."
- To which she said, "We emigrated because of you, you owe us."
- To which I said, "You only have one child."
- To which she replied, "You went back for your scarf" and pushed me forward.

Because I had no choice I approached the man and in a quiet voice said, "Parlo Italiano." He stopped screaming for a second and glared at me.

"Che cosa?" he asked in a normal voice. I considered it a win that he didn't scream at me and I told him I could help. He immediately enlisted me as his assistant, and for the next five minutes we went from one group of émigrés to another and I interpreted his instructions which basically consisted of (1) pick up your suitcases and (2) get on the buses right over there. When we were done, he shook my hand, said, "Molto grazie," and I felt like I was halfway to completing my vision board. Then I boarded the bus myself and everyone clapped and my parents shed a few tears and I thought that was a good moment to ask them for an advance on my allowance because my vision board called for a better wardrobe. They disagreed and said no.

In Italy, we had our first market economy lesson, namely: when demand outpaces supply, vision boards don't work but rules #1 and #4 still apply. I'm not an economist so don't quote me on this, but if you take the number of apartments available in Ladispoli[7] and divide that by the number of émigré arrivals, you'll get several rich scalpers and a lot of former Soviet people who no longer want to be Soviet but have to be because otherwise they'd find themselves homeless. After we'd traversed Ladispoli for days and concluded that the only thing we could afford was a bench in a park, utilities not included, my father suggested looking in the neighboring town of Santa Marinella. There was only one problem: the town's mayor didn't want any Russians living there. And because he made his ban clear to the Hebrew Immigration Aid Society (HIAS), which gave us an allowance towards our living expenses, any émigré renting in Santa Marinella would automatically forego that allowance.

This is what in English you'd call "being stuck between a rock and a hard place" and in Russian we call "nothing that can't be fixed because we're used to shit like this." Along with hundreds of others, my parents rented a flat in Santa Marinella, registered with the HIAS as living in Ladispoli, and called it a day. I acted as an interpreter with the realtor, got to practice more of my Italian to the admiring glances of my former compatriots, and figured that even if following those Soviet rules while no longer Soviet set me back from my

---

7 A town north of Rome known at the end of 1989 as the place where your rental hopes came to die. Every émigré aspired to live there, mainly because we were still a herd but also because the HIAS (Hebrew Immigration Aid Society) and the JOINT (American Jewish Joint Distribution Committee), the two organizations sponsoring our exodus, had their offices there and it's always wise to be close to the command center.

33

vision board goal, at least it got me to speak Italian so maybe it was a fair trade. Two weeks after we moved in, the mayor lifted the ban. I'd like to think it was because he saw the errors of his exclusionary ways, but it was probably because it was winter and we were good for the economy in a town where no Italian wanted to stay post beach weather. More importantly though, none of us got caught and my mother finally stopped reminding me that I went back for my scarf.

PS: I still look in the mirror if I come back after leaving.

PPS: And I still have that scarf.

PPPS: It's been more than three decades.

IMMIGRATION PART 2, OR HOW TO ASSIMILATE AHEAD OF SCHEDULE

Italy became the very first Western country in which we actually lived or—as it was known in our house—ran a household while (1) saving on the electricity bill by unplugging the refrigerator at night and rationing showers, (2) saving on groceries by standing in front of the pasta shelf to figure out which pasta was cheaper among the 369 brands available, and (3) saving on clothing purchases and future, US-based domestic expenses by appropriating whatever clothes and home items the landlord had left behind and squeezing them into our suitcases.[1] And because it's good to get ahead in your homework and I've always been a decent student, I figured that assimilating into the US would be easier if I used my time in Italy to become as Western as possible. Here are some of the strategies I tried (and some that I didn't but really wanted to).

MAKE WESTERN FRIENDS

This didn't come easy because most Italians my age didn't live in our dead-in-the-winter resort town, and those who did already had plenty of friends. But I was thankful for the few older men who always wanted to befriend me and, because it allowed me to practice

---

1 Finders keepers, right? I mean, why would you leave behind a per-fectly good shirt and two blankets (which, incidentally, my mother *still* has 30 years later) if you want them?

my Italian, I sometimes agreed to meet them in a pizzeria. Then I showed up with my parents who appreciated the opportunity to try real pizza and also my kindness in bringing them along. The older Italian men didn't appreciate that.

And then there was this one time I thought I'd struck gold when a group of "Jews for Jesus" arrived from the US to compete with the Lubavitch contingent who disembarked before them and was already gaining ground in the contest for the affections, lost souls, and future donations of Soviet Jews. The "Jews for Jesus" group brought with them young people who were eager to convert us but also to explore Rome. I spent several days in the company of one such young man practicing English, admiring the Trevi Fountain and the Spanish Steps, and hoping that learning the Jesus vocabulary was going to help me understand Americans. (It didn't. Not really. Or at least not until the evangelicals helped elect Trump.)

UPGRADE THE WARDROBE

We all arrived in Italy with bulging luggage. Not because we had to squeeze our entire previous lives into the two suitcases per person the Soviet government graciously allowed us to take, but because we had to squeeze our entire previous lives into them *plus* allow space for smoked sausage to supplement our diets, and a collection of Soviet trinkets to supplement our allowances. A street market in Rome named "Americano"[2] was one of the places to sell these trinkets, and

---

2 Because nostalgia is always a great tour guide, I went back to look for this market when I was in Rome in 2015. NO ONE I asked had ever heard of it. The locals kept asking if I meant a watered-down espresso

together with other émigrés we'd take a train and then a bus there, dragging along our collection of paraphernalia everyone said Italians would spend their hard-earned liras on. That collection was carefully researched, curated, and based on the instructions sent by the émigrés who came before us. As such, our blanket of trinkets included:

- Zhostovo metal platters guaranteed to woo an Italian mamma who just had to serve her home-made ravioli on them.
- Palekh lacquer boxes featuring motifs of Russian winter, depicting scenes from Russian fairytales, and showcasing portraits of Lenin. (That last one? *Not* sold and is now sitting on a shelf in my parents' guest bedroom.)
- Octoberists' lapel pins with a young, pudgy-faced Lenin who apparently looked just like young Oleksandr Zavarov, a famous Soviet footballer (sold out in one day to the excited group of young Italians chanting "piccolo Zavarov, piccolo Zavarov!").
- Komandirskie wrist watches backed by the full faith and credit of the Red Army—preferably the ones with a Kremlin-like star instead of the number 12 for a more authentic feeling and, therefore, a few more liras.
- A pair of pointe shoes we couldn't for the life of us sell *anywhere*.

I accompanied my parents to that market not out of the goodness of my heart or because I wanted to help them sell. It was mostly driven by the answer I got when I approached them about revamping

---

and I kept answering that the memories I came to revisit dated back to 1989 and the world of coffee was not yet that fancy.

my wardrobe by visiting a few of the local boutiques and sinking approximately ten times an average Soviet salary into a pair of jeans I found hot. Their answer sounded something like "Are you out of your mind? Go take the trash out and absolutely not, clothes are not our priority!" Since I didn't give up easily—and especially when such important things as dreams of an improved me wearing jeans were concerned—I convinced them that it was only fair to pay me commission if I went with them to Americano and sold a few things. What I did with my commission was obviously my business and since I oversold all of our competitors using my fluent Italian, they didn't argue. I spent every lira I made on a dark green velvety blazer with silky lining—hands down the most beautiful thing I've ever laid eyes on (and the most expensive thing I've ever owned). My parents pointed out it was also the most irresponsible thing I'd ever done, but I disagreed because clearly they didn't understand the importance of clothes in transformations.

AVOID GOING TO *SKHODKA*

Skhodka was the late-80s Russian immigrant real-life version of a Facebook group with only one administrator, no moderators, and everyone shouting over one another. And by everyone I mean every émigré who lived in Santa Marinella pre- and post-ban; if I were being conservative that would amount to a few million people, give or take a thousand. Now picture them roaming together in one giant crowd in a small park near the town's train station every evening around seven. They were there to meet a train from

Ladispoli that delivered a HIAS messenger, who after descending from his iron chariot and climbing on a bench, supposedly to be better heard but also to appear more important,[3] would tell them everything they needed to know about their immigration process. This basically amounted to him reading *aloud for everyone to hear* the names of everyone who: (1) passed or hadn't passed the AIDS test (what is privacy?); (2) succeeded or hadn't succeeded in securing refugee status from the US Immigration and Naturalization Service which—and I'm being 100 percent sincere here—was basically a life or death situation; and (3) had received a sponsorship from either a relative or a Jewish community in the US, Canada, or Australia and was about to leave behind the putrid pile of misery that *skhodka* had become after a thousand-year-long immigration process. To *skhodka*, people came with hope. From *skhodka*, people returned sobbing, pensive, terrified, and very rarely happy. Add to this the fact that everyone there was an émigré and I was trying to hone my status as a Westerner and you'll understand why I didn't want to be there.

GET A JOB

In the Soviet Union, it was unheard of for a young person to hold any kind of job before acquiring some kind of proof—namely, a university or a vocational college degree a.k.a. the greatest communist education in the world—that they were able to join our great

---

3 The visual you want to imagine here is a painting of Lenin addressing the masses from a podium or a tank, or some kind of battleship.

communist economy and not mess it up.[4] Getting a job in Italy wasn't just getting my first job in the West, it was also getting my first job ever. Don't quote me on this because memory is no longer my strong suit, but I think I may have been the only Russian émigré under 21 to work while in immigration.

The job in question was that of interpreter to an Italian doctor who was contracted by the HIAS to see Russian patients. Until I applied for it, the position was held by émigrés who spoke no Italian (and barely any English, which didn't matter anyway because the doctor *only* spoke Italian). But they knew a guy who knew another guy who knew the previous interpreter who was finally leaving for their long-awaited future and was now willing to sell the job like his first month of rent in America depended on it. All jobs among the Russian Jewish émigré community in Italy were closely controlled by what we called the "émigré mafia." They did their best to emulate the Italian mafia, because just like the rest of us, they'd watched *La Piovra*, which aired in the Soviet Union before we all emigrated, and it's always good to have aspirations.

I didn't think I'd get that job. Mainly because this kind of lucky break happened to me exactly never, and also because we didn't

---

4 The exception was volunteering to build BAM which stood for Baikalo-Amurskaya Magistral, which was Russian for "some railroad the Soviets were building in the far east" and teenager for "romantic adventure far far away from your parents who'd no longer be able to tell you what to do." My friends and I discussed signing up for it but then decided against it because it's hard work to build a railroad from scratch.

know anyone in the mafia and didn't have money for a bribe. But three things happened simultaneously when I applied: (1) I was the only applicant who spoke Italian; (2) the stars aligned in exactly the way they'd never align in my life again; and (3) the doctor called the organization that had sent him all the previous interpreters and, in no uncertain terms, told them he was no longer willing to speak with his hands when he really needed those hands to examine his patients. He added that if they wanted him to continue seeing their émigré pool they better send him someone who at least knew some Italian, and no, by "some" he didn't mean "*ciao*," "*grazie*," and "*va a fanculo*."

I'm proud to report that after I was hired the doctor only had to speak with his hands once. This happened when he said the word *supposta* and I had no idea what it meant (in my defense, medical terminology wasn't my expertise—selling Soviet trinkets and organizing immigrants on station platforms were). After repeating the word again but still failing to make me understand what it meant, he lifted his body off the chair a little and with a smile that looked as uncomfortable as his possibly burning thighs he pointed to the back of his pants. Which confused me even more but then, finally, both to the relief of his thighs and my self-respect as a budding but professional interpreter, I got it and now this is one of the Italian words that's been seared into my brain. The Sunday after that incident I convinced my father to buy me a heavy Russian-Italian dictionary at Americano and spent my free time studying medical terminology to avoid more hand gestures lest they endangered my job and my clear future as a 100 percent Westerner.

TRAVEL AROUND ITALY WITH A HOT ITALIAN THE LIKES OF
ADRIANO CELENTANO, TOTO CUTUGNO, OR ANY OTHER
SANREMO MUSIC FESTIVAL STARS OF THE LATE-STAGE USSR

My inspiration for this strategy came from a trip my parents and
I took to Florence and Venice on a bus chartered for the émigrés.
Everyone on it was Russian— except for a couple of Italian beaus
accompanying two young women about my age who came sans
their parents and were completely unbothered by all the shaming
looks their unmarried, sinful couplings were eliciting from the
rest of their compatriots. I envied them—not only because they
strolled along the romantic Venetian canals hand in hand with their
handsome lovers while I lugged behind my parents hoping to go
unnoticed (because traveling with chaperones when you're 20 is
just not sexy), but also because they did this as if it was the most
natural thing in the world. They felt *zero* shame despite a coordi-
nated chorus of Russian *babushkas'* sighs and my mother 's insistent
once-overs. They were my heroes. I spent the entire three days of that
holiday wishing I too could grow the backbone required to disappoint my parents, disavow shame, and embrace that free thinking
that Westerners were known for and those girls were practicing in
full view. I'd hoped to do so by finding a handsome Italian to hold
my hand as we sold Soviet souvenir trinkets at a midnight bazaar
in Rimini[5] to raise some badly needed funds for Venetian bellinis.

---

5 I actually never did this, both because of the absence of the sexy
   Italian and because Rimini was the only place we ever stayed in a
   hotel, and hot showers were unlimited, free, and didn't require rationing. I spent the entire night in the shower.

Spoiler alert: I never found a handsome Italian to disappoint my parents with.

Another spoiler alert: It happened. Eventually. (Not the handsome Italian but the disappointing the parents bit.)

IF YOU CANNOT TRAVEL WITH AN ITALIAN, EAT CAKE LIKE AN ITALIAN

The first thing I did after I collected my first paycheck was to walk into the bakery located right underneath our communal apartment and ask them if they had the 11,000-lira cake (about $9 at 1990 exchange rates and about a week's worth of wages for me) I'd heard about. To which the shopkeeper answered no. I went back with the same question the next day, and the day after that, and the day after that. And then, like that money was burning a hole in my pocket of a size diametrically opposed to my rapidly diminishing self-worth, I went back several more times.

Before you judge me on what my husband now calls my "inability to take no for an answer," you need to understand the following:

1) We lived above that bakery and woke up to the smell of freshly baked pastries, cookies, and cakes *every day*. We then had to inhale that fairytale aroma for the rest of the day while living on a diet of stale bread, mashed potatoes, and discounted pasta.
2) We didn't dare to enter the premises because all of the bakery's clients were Italian and most of them were elderly signoras who wore fur coats when it wasn't even cold. What were the chances we could afford anything there *ever*? Answer: None.

3) Then one time a couple of émigrés told me they heard the bakery carried a cake for 11,000 liras and it was the cheapest cake there.

4) I nourished that grapevine intelligence as if it was a plastic bag with foreign writing, a.k.a. a Soviet Birkin Bag, until I got a job and while I waited for a week to get paid, which honestly felt like a year.

5) I wasn't going to give up on a dream, because what else do we have if we don't have dreams?

The 763rd time I walked into that bakery and prepared to ask the same question the shopkeeper smiled at me and said: "We don't have an 11,000-lira cake today." Then, before I could make a U-ie to hide my rapidly burning cheeks, he continued, pointing to a fruit tart with kiwis, strawberries, and mandarin slices: "But we have a 12,000-lira cake." I thought for a second, then dug into my pockets, and produced 12,000 liras. The shopkeeper wrapped the cake with a bow, put it on the counter in front of me, counted out 11,000 liras, then slid 1,000 back to me, and smiled. I died of embarrassment and got out of there much faster than it had taken me to translate *supposta*.

By the end of our stay in Italy I had accumulated enough second-hand knock-offs from Americano to pass for an Italian, had been to *skhodka* exactly two times of the expected 198, and spoke Italian with a Roman-enough accent to fool the doctor's Italian clients who I chatted up while waiting for my Russian patients in his lobby. "Where did you learn to speak Russian so well?" they asked me. I smiled and did not correct them because disappointing sweet old ladies isn't something I take lightly. Besides, if with their combined years of experience in the West they'd decided I was Italian, who was I to argue? Especially since it meant I'd succeeded in my transformation into a Westerner way ahead of schedule and without a hot Italian by my side. Which was definitely something to be proud of.

WHAT'S IN A NAME?

Can you name the feeling when you're on a plane, rushing through the air at God knows how many miles an hour, and you're exhausted because this is your second flight and your first one was crossing the Atlantic (the one and only long-haul flight you've ever taken), and you have very little understanding of what's going on around you because your English does not yet exist, and then a flight attendant comes along with her cart and offers you your very first can of Coca Cola? With a smile? And *for free*?

If you answered relief, you're wrong.

A friend who's very much into self-improvement said gratitude but that's wrong too, because back in 1990 nobody cared about gratitude and everyone was very much like, "Give me this Coca Cola, it's my right." I'm projecting, of course, because I didn't think like that, not yet anyway. That's because my only prior experience of flying was Aeroflot and the only free thing you ever got on those flights was a scowl and, possibly, a fiery crash.

But I digress.

The only correct answer to the question posed in the first paragraph is *freedom*. At least, that was the only correct answer for me because I cannot, of course, speak for my parents, who were probably occupied with wondering how to open their cans but also whether they could keep them closed and carry them off the plane (you'd understand that if you spent your childhood, adolescence, and mature years drinking *gazirovka*—a fizzy, something-flavored water available from machines at metro stations and served in a reusable glass everyone drank out of).

I drank the whole can of Coke and it tasted sweet, of caramel, and tingly. All descriptors for freedom, obviously. Also potential precursors to the 16 dental appointments I would have in the first year of my life in America, each one for a cavity I didn't get because I drank too much soda but *did* get because I grew up in the Soviet Union where anesthesia and dentistry weren't considered a good match. It was clearly a ploy by the Communist Party to develop super humans, because if you could survive the drill without Novocain you could survive anything. Spoiler alert: the ploy failed and we were mostly just people with bad teeth and a lot of vodka in our freezers for toothache self-medication.

But back to the Coke.

That sweet taste told me I'd made it to America. Of course, I already knew that, seeing as I was on a plane from New York to New Hampshire, but drinking that sugary concoction of ingredients we aren't allowed to know told me I'd really made it. As in: my former life as a Soviet-born-and-bred person with bad teeth was now completely over and a new me, an American me (still with bad teeth), was occupying this seat thousands of meters (oops, feet now) up in the air.

What do you think I did with this realization?

If you answered "implement changes to your life immediately" you'd be right. (If you answered get another can of Coke, you'd be right too.) I'd decided on my list of changes while still in Moscow— and I perfected that list while in immigration in Italy—because I like to be prepared and also because I planned to turn into an

American the moment I crossed into American airspace. Which, in retrospect, was a bit of wishful thinking, because while flying over the Atlantic I couldn't really tell when we did that. I thought of asking a flight attendant but then I couldn't decide how to phrase the question and I didn't want it to sound too Russian. Because that would defeat the entire purpose.

I had four items on my list of changes:

1) Get a pair of Levi's (because according to every Soviet adolescent, you weren't fully American if you didn't own Levi's).
2) Get an education in anything but engineering (because according to every Soviet Jew, Jewish people could study whatever they wanted in America).
3) Find an American boyfriend/husband (because according to me, dating and marrying any of my former compatriots meant marrying my father).
4) Learn to speak English without a hint of a Russian accent (because the Russian accent just sounds crude; there is nothing sexy or remotely attractive about it).

When we landed in New York I tried to get a head start on that list and asked my parents for the money for (1) but, just like in Italy, they weren't too impressed with me being this much in a hurry to shop. They also didn't think it was wise to spend the little savings we had on jeans. Which, obviously, they were wrong about because those weren't just *jeans*, they were *Levi's* and they were going to turn me into an American. Honestly, I don't know how they didn't understand the significance of that.

But I didn't have much time to sulk about this in New York, because after signing 553 pieces of paper promising to behave in America (at least that's what I think they were about; I didn't really pay attention, there were too many beautiful people with good teeth wearing Levi's to gawk at), we were sent on to our connecting flight to New Hampshire, where my life as an American would commence.

Because my parents didn't give me money for the Levi's and because my other changes weren't easily implementable while strapped into a seat at 33,000 feet up in the air, I decided that I needed to come up with another item for my list of changes. That item had to be actionable on the spot, would have to make an American out of me immediately, and would need to be so impressive that those meeting us at the Manchester airport in New Hampshire would immediately agree I was the most American of all Russian émigrés they had ever met.

In the Soviet Union, we had a proverb, *Kak vstretish novi god tak ego y provedesh*, which translated as, "The way you celebrate New Year's Eve will be the way you'll spend your new year" and was basically invented to compete in the New Year's Eve party Olympics. Which was really a lot of pressure because I wasn't the most popular kid in school and all of my invitations to New Year's Eve parties were either lost in the Soviet mail (which was very likely) or never sent at all (even more likely). That meant I celebrated each New Year's Eve with my family, which actually wasn't that bad. Mainly because my *babushka* made a mean baked duck stuffed with apples, but also because I could claim to anyone who asked that I considered New Year's Eve a family holiday. But seriously, I think because I always went to my grandparents' apartment and didn't party with

49

lots of cool kids, I never became a cool kid the following year. Which means the proverb was 100 percent correct and even though we wouldn't be celebrating New Year's Eve when we landed, it would still be the beginning of something—namely *my life in America*—and I needed to make sure I did it right. (Although not the same kind of "right" as the year I was too fed up clinking champagne glasses with my family instead of those cool kids, so I protested by staying at home, celebrating alone, and toasting with milk. This, of course, resulted in me missing the best cuts of the duck and also in having even fewer cool friends the following year.)

All that to say, starting my life in America the right way meant it had to go well from the very start, and that was a lot of pressure. Especially if you consider another Soviet proverb, *Vstrechauyt po odezhke, provozhayut po umu*, which means, "People form their impressions of you based on what you're wearing when you first meet, but they remember you by your intelligence." Which, honestly, was a load of crap because good clothes were such a rarity in the Soviet Union that if you wore something decent (read: clothing made outside the USSR) everyone remembered you for *that* and not for whatever math theorem you were the first to prove. But because I was not traveling in Levi's I could pretty much be assured that the people meeting us at the airport would get a totally wrong impression of me (read: not see me as the most American of all Russian émigrés they'd ever met) and the beginning of my life in America would commence on completely the wrong foot and I would never be or become a real American. Ever.

Then we landed and got our luggage, and I realized that all of my dreams about turning into an American right there and then were on serious life support. Because, honestly, who would ever think of me as an American with suitcases that looked as if they'd gone through several Russian revolutions? (To be fair, despite its sorry state, our luggage would probably have had an easier time being classified as "the most Western of all luggage belonging to Russian émigrés" than I ever would in the human category equivalent. My parents tapped into all of their *blat* and spent a lot of money in Moscow to procure the best Chinese-made suitcases that roubles could buy. And at that time in the Soviet luggage world, "Made in China" was the equivalent of Levi's in the Soviet jeans world.)

Then something happened that I thought of as an opportunity, and my father thought of as *Chert voz'mi, y teper' chto*, which loosely translates to "Now what the hell are we going to do?"

The airport was deserted. This ordinarily wouldn't have been a problem, but it was for us because it looked like no one had come to meet us.

FATHER [looking around the deserted baggage claim area]: Now what are we going to do?

GRANDFATHER: Maybe they confused our flight?

MOTHER [looking around the deserted baggage claim area]: This was the only flight and it's two o'clock in the morning. Maybe they forgot about us?

FATHER: That's great. Just great.

ME [rejoicing that I had some extra time to figure out how to turn myself into an American]: Maybe they're late. Or maybe they're waiting somewhere else.

FATHER: I'm going to take a walk and look around.

MOTHER: I'll go with you.

GRANDFATHER: Me too.

FATHER [to me]: Rita, grab your suitcase, let's go.

That was an order and, honestly, I didn't mind obeying it because I wasn't going to just stand there alone with all of our ugly suitcases while my family walked around the airport. But the fact that my father basically did what he'd always done—told me what to do—gave me a eureka moment. I suddenly knew then and there how I was going to turn myself into an American before even leaving the baggage claim.

I was going to change my name.

Not change it completely but update it. Kind of like those computer updates we all install to get rid of bugs. (Although in those days the only computer I'd ever seen was a machine that took up several rooms in a Moscow Research Institute where my friend and I were sent during our last year of high school for an internship-type practical experience. We spent the time feeding punch cards into that machine with the goal of having a curve printed on a large sheet of paper. I still have no idea why anyone needed that curve printed when it was much easier to just draw it, but I remember feeling all smug because our other classmates were interning at a bakery and actually had to work.)

To be clear, my name had no bugs in it, but it did have a lot of baggage. And that baggage—much like the actual baggage we arrived with—had to go if I were to become an American as soon as possible.

I'm not a psychologist or a linguist, but somehow I realized that if I kept going by the same name as I did in the Soviet Union, not only would I NOT leave that airport as an American, I would NEVER become fully American. Not because my name sounded Russian, but because it sounded Russian to *me*. You know when you eat a bad egg and then puke it all out, the taste of that bad egg is forever embedded in your taste buds and you can't look at eggs the same way for a long, long time (if ever)? It's the same idea. Hearing someone call me Rita would be like tasting that egg over and over again, with the egg standing in for shit I hated while living in the Soviet Union, namely:

- Elaborate rules on how a "good girl" was supposed to behave. Those rules included but were not limited to: always listening to your parents; never crossing any *babushka* sat near your building for the sole purpose of provoking you to cross her; not kissing a boy until he spent years pursuing you—and even then making it look like you weren't enjoying it; not having sex before marriage—and even after that making it look like you weren't enjoying it; and not wearing anything short ever (because that wasn't decent Komsomol behavior and also because you didn't have the legs for it).
- Elaborate rules on how a "good Jewish girl" was supposed to behave. Those rules included but were not limited to: listening to your mother on who to date and who to marry; obeying your family (but mostly your father) on what to study; then obeying the Politburo and studying engineering (because that was a safe profession to entrust to Jews); and obeying your local Komsomol charter because that was the rule of the majority and who were you to disagree?

To sum up the above: growing up in the Soviet Union as a young Jewish woman basically meant being ordered around by everyone—your parents, the Communist Party, *babushkas*, store clerks, Komsomol leaders, and dentists.

Because, to me, America was the land of freedom and I had just drunk two whole cans of it, I dragged my suitcase behind me and vowed that I would never again go by the name Rita. Then we turned the corner and saw a group of people standing in a circle in an empty hallway. They were in the midst of a very animated discussion, so animated that they were completely oblivious to the only other humans in their vicinity—us—and also to the machine that was attempting to get around them to clean the floor.

GRANDFATHER: Are these people here for us?

FATHER: [turning his head upside down in an attempt to read the sign—also upside down—that one of these people was holding behind his back while swinging it back and forth]: It says, *Dobro pozhalovat*. They must be.

Because we quickly concluded that we were the only people in the airport to whom those two Russian words for "welcome" would have any kind of meaning, we dragged our suitcases towards the group. They still didn't notice us.

FATHER [in a heavy Russian accent]: Are you waiting for us?

ALL OF US [smiling awkwardly]

THEM [lots of exclaiming and many English sentences I didn't understand but deduced the meaning to be *Oh no, we must have missed the announcement for your flight and how long have you been waiting and we are so very sorry and it is so nice to meet you and here, read*: Dobro Pozhalovat *right side up*].

Then everyone started shaking hands and saying their names, and this is when I knew the moment of my most important introduction had arrived.

ME: My name is Margarita.

That was after my father introduced himself as Vladimir, my mother as Inessa, and my *dedushka* as Israel (all longer, formal versions of their first names). Which honestly should have made it much easier for them to accept my calling myself "Margarita" instead of the usual "Rita" because "Margarita" IS the formal version of "Rita." But it didn't. Probably because they all considered themselves adults and I was still a child. At 21 years old.

My mother threw me the most incredulous look ever, which basically said "What are you trying to pull, quit it" and my father ignored my introduction and continued to call me Rita. At this point the Americans got confused and asked if I was Rita or Margarita or something else entirely, and I had to explain that in Russian "Rita" was short for "Margarita" but that I'd like to be called "Margarita" from now on, thank you very much.

Which is when my mother pursed her lips and took her first offense in America. She was scandalized at how easily I threw away the past and *everything* that made me. Honestly, I couldn't understand how she didn't see that throwing away that *everything* was why I wanted to come to America in the first place. But for her this was treason. Mostly because she (and my father) didn't agree to it. And because every decision I made had to have their stamp of approval. And because that's how things always worked, so what was wrong with me?

PS: My parents still call me Rita (30 years later).

HOW TO DO JEWISH RIGHT

When coming of age as a Jewish girl in the USSR, you had several concerns to deal with on a daily basis:

1) Does my last name sound Jewish?
2) Does it sound more Jewish than that other guy's in my class?
3) Is he Jewish or is he just unlucky enough to have a Jewish last name without actually being Jewish?
4) Does my nose look Jewish?
5) What about in profile?
6) Do my eyes bulge out?[1]
7) Did this boy just call me *zhidovka* because he likes me?
8) Does he keep calling me this because he still likes me?
9) How do I keep it together when my class is discussing how Fanya Kaplan shot Lenin and everyone is staring at me because she was Jewish?
10) How do I keep it together when the class is discussing the evil capitalism of Israel and everyone is staring at me because I'm the only Jew in this class?

---

1 Most of my Soviet compatriots could name the main antisemitic stereotypes—hooked nose, bulging eyes, thick and wavy hair—better than they could recite the words to the national anthem. Which is kind of understandable when you think about it, since the anthem wasn't as popular as antisemitism.

11) Do I risk a break-up served with a heavy dose of *zhidovka* if I date this Russian boy I like?

12) There are no attractive Jewish boys anywhere so perhaps I'll risk it.

13) Wrong decision. So wrong.

14) Where do I hide?

When you immigrate to the US as a young Jewish woman from the Soviet Union, you have the following concerns:

1) Am I doing this right?

2) What's a *dreidel*?

Until about halfway into the third grade I had a pretty normal Soviet childhood. Get up in the morning, eat a cheese sandwich, walk to school, show your change of shoes at the door,[2] take your place in the second row of your classroom, get selected to be the captain of your Little Red Star group, use recess to organize your Little Red Star group to work on a poster for the upcoming celebration of the Russian Revolution, join the rest of your elementary school to learn to march like a Red Army soldier for the school parade during the said celebration, and avoid the school bathroom at all costs unless that was the day you practiced your Cold War defense and had a gas mask to wear. In the third grade, though, it was time to become

---

2 You couldn't enter your school building unless you offered proof that you brought "indoor shoes" to change into. No, our school hallways weren't laid with Italian marble. Yes, our janitor *babushkas* were ruthless.

MARGARITA GOKUN SILVER

devious. That deviousness included challenging authority, which for a nine-about-to-turn-ten-year-old meant sneaking into the teacher's journal while the teacher was out during recess.

The goal was to learn the grades we'd received for some previous test and I was completely on board with that. Until the boys who were running the show turned to the first page of the journal and stopped dead with excitement.

"Look!" One of them practically squealed in delight pointing his finger with a dirty, bitten nail at me. "She's a Jewess!"

Everyone stared. My first thought was: *Chto zdes' proiskhodit?*, which today could be translated as *WTF?* My second thought was: *Why are they looking at me like there's something wrong me? Do I have a booger sticking out of my nose or something?* My third thought was: *What is a Jewess?*

If you're surprised that a nine-year-old Jewish child didn't know she was Jewish, don't be. I'm surprised at this myself now, but that's because I raised my daughter to be proudly Jewish, sent her to a Jewish day school and then to Hebrew school, and paid for a large gathering of family members to witness her become a Bat Mitzvah and then dance the night away on a dance floor filled with 13-year-olds. My daughter knew she was Jewish the moment my husband told her about the Holocaust when she was *two*. (He didn't hold back either, gas chambers were front and center in that story, I kid you not. For the record, I wasn't on board. I thought he could have waited until she turned three.) In contrast, I didn't know I was Jewish until that boy pointed at me and shared my ethnicity with the whole class because he was proud he could read and that information was readily available in the teacher's journal.

From the moment I was "discovered" as a Jew, things pretty much went downhill for me. The taunting was daily and real, the institutionalized and systemic antisemitism was real, the animosity and jeering at bus stops and in queues were real. On the plus side, if quantum physics was my jam, I could have probably invented an invisibility cloak because in both my school and, later, at university I pretty much aced the art of being invisible. It helped that I didn't look Jewish and that my last name didn't sound Jewish,[3] and that I successfully contributed to the aura of my persona *not-being* Jewish by never mentioning the subject, never speaking up against antisemitic utterances, and completely ignoring that part of myself like it was the elephant in the room if the elephant stood for the second-class citizen status bestowed on us at birth and the room stood for our supposedly equal Motherland.

Then Gorbachev's policy of *glasnost* made all kinds of bigotry okay to print. The freedom of speech vibe was worth it for a while—or until someone suggested we keep the lights off in our apartment on a certain night because that was the night a mob of antisemites, bent on weeding out the Jews, was supposed to sweep through Moscow.

---

3 If recognizing an Ashkenazi Jew had been a competitive sport, Russians would have won all the medals for it in the antisemitism Olympics without even practicing. But my last name was Sephardic and I suppose this is as good a time as any to thank Isabella and Ferdinand for kicking my grandfather's ancestors out of Spain in the fifteenth century and, thus, saving me from some of that Russian vitriol. Which, I realize, is kind of ironic because if they hadn't been kicked out, then I wouldn't have had to grow up in the Soviet Union and wouldn't have had to avoid that vitriol in the first place.

That didn't seem like a healthy way to discuss our differences, or even a good prelude to finding ways to get our Soviet family of disenfranchised ethnicities together and save the country from the sinkhole towards which it was heading. Besides, I wasn't going to do the saving if my people were being blamed for all of this destruction. Hello, they took part in the Revolution just like everyone else but constituted *only* about two percent of the population, so how much blame did that really warrant? Meanwhile my *dedushka*'s nephew sent letters from the US singing the praises of its freedom of religion (while also extolling the virtues of capitalism), and our completely non-religious family decided it was time to figure out what being Jewish meant, aside from being derided, hated, and blamed for a poor collective farm harvest.

I need to point out here that most Soviet Jews I knew—or had heard about—weren't religious. In our family, the only proof that being Jewish meant having some kind of relationship with God (aside from being the chosen people to accept the abuse our compatriots leveled at us) was my *dedushka* fasting on Yom Kippur and crisscrossing Moscow before Passover in search of matzo.[4] He never explained any of this to me, but maybe that was because I didn't bother to ask since I was too busy being a disciplined atheist whose idea of God came from Karl Marx[5] and also from our neighbor at the dacha, the wife of a Russian Orthodox priest, who prayed every

---

4 This was the same grandfather who ate *vetchina*, or Russian ham, but such were the contradictions of being a Soviet Jew and also of not having much choice in the cold cuts department of Soviet grocery stores.

5 Karl Marx said "Religion is the opium of the people." He lived before Netflix.

morning at 6 a.m., waking me up[6] and thus cementing my conclusion that believing in God wasn't really my thing.

The first Jewish holiday we celebrated properly was Passover. It happened in Italy during immigration, and by properly I mean we *almost* made it to the end of the Haggadah reading before we broke down and started sneaking hard-boiled eggs and matzo under the table. In our defense, no one explained that we should have eaten before we showed up to what was advertised as a Passover *dinner*; because why would you eat if you'd been promised a free dinner and could therefore save your leftover pasta for the next day? We walked in to see long tables set up with large round plates with edible items, and maybe when they started the service they mentioned we weren't supposed to eat those just yet but I don't remember that. For a while there we were disciplined and behaved in a really cultured way as we waited for the hosts to start the meal, but when, half an hour later, it became apparent that at the head of the table they were clearly occupied with reading something in Hebrew none of us understood, the sound of hard-boiled eggs being cracked under the tables filled the room. On the plus side, that dinner was the first time I tried gefilte fish and I can tell you with 100 percent certainty that it's a fish with potato aspirations and that's just weird.

In America, we were fully expected to attend services in a synagogue because the committee that volunteered to welcome us to the US was founded in that synagogue. Obviously, we didn't want to disappoint our hosts, so off we went to the Shabbat services every Friday evening and there we leafed through the *siddurs* like we were born

6 Those walls were really thin.

to do it until someone pointed out we had to start at the end of the book and turn those pages in the opposite direction. My grandfather sat in the front row and attempted to learn Hebrew using his limited knowledge of Yiddish; my father sat in the back row and, like the good atheist he was raised to be, questioned every reference to God; and I sat wherever was closer to the room where they served what they called *kiddish* and I called "the new kind of American cookies to try."

That lasted for a few weeks or until my parents moved to Ohio. On arrival, they gleefully reported there were no synagogues in their tiny town and so they went back to being Jewish the way they understood it—with ham in their fridge and without any praying on Friday nights. My *dedushka* moved to Los Angeles and could now pray in Russian, which was a relief both for him and his new American friends who didn't count on having to teach an old man English while ingesting those *kiddish* cookies. And I stopped going to services because there was singing involved and I was completely tone deaf. Plus, I didn't know any of the words so I couldn't even make it look as if I was singing the way I'd done when the choir teacher had chosen five-year-old me to stand in the front row on account of my face being *very expressive*. "Just don't sing out loud," he'd told me. "Mouth it."

But, honestly, it wasn't just the singing. The whole concept of a God, of some higher power, sitting up there and deciding to dispense punishment if you didn't pray hard enough or if you didn't show up for services or if you showed up only to see what kind of cookies they were serving that evening, was completely foreign to me. I just couldn't buy into the idea that I was subject to someone else's power, someone who seemed almost as fickle as those medieval lords towering over their serfs—and didn't we get rid of those in 1917? Also, I could just sin to my heart's content and then admit it and get off that easily? I mean, even the Communist Party wasn't that lenient, and we were talking about an omnipotent being that had more than gulags at his disposal. And why was it always "He"? Why not "She"? If no one had ever seen the deity we prayed to, why were we using the male pronoun? Didn't we have enough of the old men patriarchy here on Earth?

Since I was new to this whole religion thing and also because speaking up as a young immigrant was against my immigration manual, I didn't share any of this blasphemy with anyone. Instead, I decided self-righteousness was the way to go, and by that I mean I figured that if I couldn't become truly Jewish by sincerely believing everything that the *siddur* claimed had happened, I could try to become truly Jewish by criticizing whatever glaringly un-Jewish actions my parents engaged in. In other words, repeat after me: if you desperately want to join your family in celebrating the New Year by putting up a New Year's tree as you've done for years but can't now because that New Year's tree is actually a Christmas tree in America and that's fundamentally un-Jewish, then you express your displeasure at their tree by lecturing them about how to be truly Jewish. This is a topic you know nothing about but nevertheless feel indignant enough to be qualified to preach on behalf of all American Jewry of whom you don't feel part, but desperately want to.

My parents are never ones to back down, especially in an argument that comes from me since, as parents, they automatically know better and, as a child, "you don't know what you're talking about." Which is a stance I would ordinarily have a problem with, but looking back now I can grudgingly admit they had a point. The *how* of being Jewish didn't have to be defined as either one of the two extremes—the Soviet one where you were ethnically Jewish but religiously a non-believer, or the American one where you couldn't be Jewish without being able to carry the tune. But because I'd just arrived from the land of polarities, from the country where gray was the color of people's moods and not an opinion option, and from a system where "if you're not with us, you're against us" was part of the national anthem, naturally I assumed the pendulum had to swing the other way for me to belong.

I gave all of that up a few years down the road, mainly because it was exhausting to criticize my parents' annual Hanukkah bush, but also because no matter how hard I criticized and no matter how hard I tried to turn my face into a model of dramatic delight whenever I ended up in the synagogue and had to join in the singing, belonging just wasn't happening. It was almost like reverse déjà vu—as a former Soviet Jew I felt almost as foreign among American Jews as I felt being Jewish among the Russians. Hello, what? I'd emigrated because I wanted to find my people and join my tribe, but then this seemingly was never coming to be, so, huh? What was I even?

To investigate this, I decided to defy the norms I'd established for my nascent Jewishness by getting a New Year's tree when we were living back in Russia for my husband's job. My excuse was that I wanted to show my daughter what it was like to celebrate the New Year when I was a child. In lieu of my grandfather who sadly was no longer available to play Ded Moroz[7]—a role he so masterfully portrayed for the naive, seven-year-old me—I decided to hire one along with Snegurochka, a Snowmaiden character who was Ded Moroz's granddaughter and who historically tagged along because she sang better and could also do a roundelay around the tree without getting that artificial beard caught in its ornaments. My husband wasn't impressed.

HIM: You want to get a Christmas tree? For our daughter? Who's Jewish?

ME: It's not a Christmas tree, it's a New Year's tree—don't you see the difference?

HIM: What's the difference?

ME: It doesn't have angels for ornaments.

HIM: It's STILL a tree.

ME: A New Year's tree.

HIM: For me it's a Christmas tree.

ME: It doesn't have to be. Just repeat after me—it's not a Christmas tree, it's a New Year's tree.

HIM: It's not working.

ME: What if we get it on December 27? Christmas will be officially over by then and we can just agree on it being a New Year's tree.

That conversation went on for about another hour, but ended with me convincing him because I'm good with circular arguments and also probably because it was dinner time and he was hungry.

---

7 Grandfather Frost, also known as Russian Santa, but don't tell my husband because I convinced him otherwise and I don't want to revisit this topic again.

We got the tree and the ornaments and together with my daughter I decorated the tree (my husband abstained just in case the guy upstairs still thought of it as a Christmas tree). The visit by Ded Moroz and Snegurochka was a delight and my daughter went to sleep happy, singing a roundelay song about a tree and clutching a doll that looked like Snegurochka.

And then the guy—or the gal, or both, or neither—upstairs made themselves known in that fickle, medieval lord kind of way. I don't believe in comeuppance but my husband was convinced of it and so I'll recount his version of events:

That was the year I got diagnosed with breast cancer and IT WAS ALL BECAUSE OF THAT TREE. (Also because of the BRCA gene, but who needs science, right?)

I'm not going to deny this scared me a little bit. So while I sat there being infused with chemicals that were lethal if they touched my skin but were A-okay when they touched my insides, I read up on modern spirituality, on how Judaism may fit into it, and whether I could find something that said I could still call myself Jewish if I didn't fast on Yom Kippur because it gave me migraines and if I called God "Universe" and thought of it as a she. What I found sounded even better. I wish I could remember the name of the book or the author but chemo brain is real and the only thing I remember is that it was written by a rabbi. I might be misquoting or even misunderstanding, but I honestly don't care because that's exactly what I needed to fix my faltering beliefs. The book said that the divine wasn't ruling over us but was all around us—and that included *ourselves*. Which was good enough for me, because that meant God wasn't a separate being and we were all in it together and therefore He/She/They didn't give me cancer, because why would you give cancer to yourself?

Today, whenever I find myself at Friday night services, I don't pay much attention to the words nor do I try to sing (to everyone's relief). Instead I let the words wash over me and try to connect with the part that's okay with me being Jewish on my terms. Sometimes that means wondering what they're serving for *kiddish*, sometimes it involves thinking through a to-do list for the next day, and sometimes it includes STILL agonizing over whether my last name is too Jewish. Because, honestly, if the 2016 election and its subsequent racist shindig taught me anything, it is that the only way to do Jewish right is to never let your guard down.

GREAT EXPECTATIONS, THE BEGINNING

The other day I called my mother and when she answered I immediately knew something was wrong. Not in terms of her or my father's health or the water temperature in their building's pool or a recent fight one half of their condo board had with another, but I-am-upset-at-you kind of wrong. Her voice was as icy as the Siberian tundra before climate change and as distant as the past when Komsomol parades on Lenin's birthday were still a thing.

Which meant she was offended. BY ME.

I'd like to think I'm a good daughter, which is why I tried to rewind my previous conversations with her in order to understand what might have happened. But because over the years I've become really good at keeping to safe topics, it was a pretty fruitless exercise. These are my safe topics:

- Their weather.
- Our weather.
- How their weather is better than our weather but how humidity sucks.
- How our weather is almost as good as their weather but it's drier so it's actually better.
- Weather in general.

And these are the topics I've tried to stay clear of:

- My life.

I haven't shared anything of significance with either one of my parents in years. That's because I learned several important things from our immigration process:

1) If you want to know what it's like to experience a real sense of your parents' disappointment in you, get yourself a set of former-Soviet-Jewish parents.
2) That disappointment lasts and isn't easily fixed.
3) Your parents will support your aspirations only if they approve of them.
4) They'll approve of those aspirations only if three things are present: prestige, high levels of achievement, and (at least) a six-figure income.
5) If you ended up disappointing your parents and/or your aspirations never got approved, the best course of action is to never mention your life or your aspirations again and just talk about the weather.

To *not* disappoint a former-Soviet-Jewish parent you need to be a doctor, a lawyer, an investment banker, and a classical pianist of world acclaim—preferably all at the same time. If you're a girl, you're also supposed to have a perfect family of at least two children and a husband, who too is a doctor, a lawyer, or an investment banker (although he's allowed to be just *one* of those). Your house must have several crystal chandeliers, a kitchen from which delicious and nutritious meals emerge (daily, courtesy of you), and a garage with two Mercedes (or at the very least BMWs). But, most importantly, you would have acquired all this and more because you were a good girl and always listened to your parents.

Which I wasn't. And I didn't.

Although.

It's possible that quite a few years ago I may have promised to. Or maybe alluded to. Or maybe made it sound like I would? I don't know. Judge for yourself.

OUR DECISION TO IMMIGRATE
(A.K.A. THE PROMISE I'D FAIL TO KEEP: A SHORT TREATISE)

My *dedushka*'s nephew emigrated from the Soviet Union to the US in 1979 and immediately began to send letters with photos of him and his family in front of big houses and even bigger cars. (*Not* his, but we didn't know that then.)

My grandparents suggested we emigrate too.

My father refused because he had a promising career as a Soviet engineer who had to travel into the Siberian depths of the USSR to staple pieces of pipelines together, but who hoped that with enough of that stapling he'd get to travel to East Berlin or Warsaw, and maybe even more than once during his career.

Gorbachev came to power and implemented *perestroika* and *glasnost* which stood for reforms-while-still-communist and free-dom-of-speech-while-still-totalitarian.

Because of *glasnost*, antisemitism evolved from its "respectable," under-the-surface, institutionalized, run-of-the-mill animosity and discrimination into loud and in-your-face bigotry and hate.[1] Many Jews responded by packing their suitcases and also by keeping lights off in their apartments on nights when pogroms were rumored to swipe through Moscow.

Reagan got Gorbachev to agree to letting the Soviet Jewry emigrate, and my grandparents raised the subject again.

My father still refused and, seeing that my grandparents weren't getting anywhere, I joined the conversation. That was mainly because I didn't want to spend my evenings in the dark, but also because I was studying to staple pipelines and didn't envision that to be an interesting way to spend my life while hiding from antisemites.

Because I was 19 and, therefore, *still a child*, my father responded by sending me to my room and saying this was an adult topic of conversation and I had no business participating because I didn't understand life.

Obviously, he didn't know me very well.

Being called a child only made me more determined, and being sent to my room only made me more annoyed. Which made me more persistent.

I spent the next year like I was born to work on K Street. My choice of lobbying tactics included, but was not limited to: vividly describing visions of the apocalyptic future that awaited us in the Soviet Union, opportunities we could count on when we got to the

---

1 No, this isn't 2016–20 USA, it's 1985–89 USSR. Yes, Trump learned more than one lesson from Putin.

US (travel beyond East Berlin and Warsaw included), and promises I'd do whatever was in my power to make this move worth it.

The last one is where I suspect I went wrong. That's because when my father finally agreed he said, "Remember, we're doing this for you and your future." Which at that point in my family dynamic meant I was going to have to enroll into medical school as soon as we landed and make everyone proud by becoming a doctor.

That is so not what happened.

The end.

*

I abandoned all plans of ever going to medical school seven months after we arrived, while in the second semester[2] of a biology degree at a liberal arts college that had not only accepted me but also helped me with grants, transferred a year-and-a-half's worth of credits from my Moscow university,[3] and introduced me to endocrinology, which I now refer to as "the study of freedom." That's because, despite my nearly perfect English, I couldn't understand a word my

---

2 I think it was the second semester but I can't be entirely sure. My first year in the US was an intoxicating blur of supermarkets with french fries *ready for frying* (I mean potatoes peeled, then sliced, then frozen for your convenience—what kind of capitalist witchery was this?), malls with stores like Sears where, if you were smart and saved your coupons, you could find a shirt on sale for $5 and pay nothing for it because you had a $5 coupon, and also Marshalls with discounted Levi's (!).

3 That transfer included counting the History of the Communist Party as a social science credit and this is where I basically fell in love with America, but more on that later.

professor said during his first lecture. Which meant I spent an hour looking around, seeing in horror that everyone was furiously taking notes, and realizing that every single student in that class was there because they wanted to be. WITH THE EXCEPTION OF ONE.

This made me ask myself this question: Why was I doing this? And also: If I was an American now, shouldn't I exercise the freedom of choice I had heard so much about and choose my own future profession?

I walked out of that lecture, dropped endocrinology, and called my parents. Telling them they'd never have a physician in the family caused a lot of prolonged pauses and sighs, but only three questions:

1) What was I going to do with my life now?
2) How dare I not consult their opinion about making that decision?
3) How could I so cruelly treat my *babushka*'s memory?[4]

I further unimpressed them by replying "I don't know" to (1) and I answered (2) while perched high above the abyss of parental disapproval on the treacherously thin branch of the very shaky, young tree of my budding independence. "Mama, Papa," I said, "I just don't see myself being a doctor. I'm not sure I want to spend my life stuck in an office." Their profound longing for the simpler, a.k.a. stricter,

---

4 My grandmother was a doctor and it was my mother's unattainable dream that I'd honor her memory by following in her footsteps. Unattainable, because my grandmother was a doctor *ot boga*, which meant it was a God-given calling, and, obviously, I could never compare because God had me faint at the first sight of blood.

times of the Soviet parenting radiated Chernobyl-style all the way from Ohio, where they'd moved to. It was one thing to embrace democracy in a larger society, it was completely another to allow it in the family. Which is to say they expected me to remain the same obedient daughter they had raised in the USSR and to heed their opinion in all matters of my life and future.

Because feeling like a disappointment after that call wasn't the highlight of my existence (even if it came with a tub of supermarket-brand ice cream I ate right out of the tub like a *real* American), I resolved that in the future I'd try to be more considerate of their sentiments. And about a year later I thought I'd hit jackpot—while also answering questions (1) and (3) in one swoop—when I announced the course of graduate study I applied for. "International Public Health," I told them, feeling all self-satisfied that I'd managed to find a compromise. "At YALE." This was a career path they'd approve of because it honored my *babushka*'s memory; it was a profession I could potentially live with because it wouldn't encase me in a white coat and a four-walled office for the rest of my life; and it was at an Ivy League university they could brag about. Everybody wins!

My mother's answer was very effective in wiping that smug expression off my face. "What's Public Health?" she asked, ignoring the name "Yale" completely.[5] And that's when I realized that:

- a Public Health degree didn't exist in the Soviet Union and, thus, would be very hard to explain in Russian

---

5 If you still don't think impressing Soviet-Jewish parents is tough, let this sink in.

- it would *also* be hard to explain in English because I HAD NO CLEAR IDEA WHAT IT MEANT EITHER.

Now I should probably point out that my parents, my grandfather, and I had arrived in the US with huge expectations. My parents were hoping to learn English, find jobs, and figure out how to maneuver a car thrice the size of a normal Soviet vehicle on streets watched over by police who were unbribable. I was hoping to finish my education, marry an American, and buy a Ferrari.[6] My *dedushka* was hoping for all of the above and also maybe for a reliable supply of Passover matzo without having to worry about being taken in for questioning for buying it.

But the biggest of all expectations was that one day I'd wear a white coat with Dr. Gokun embroidered on the lapel, hang a stethoscope loosely around my neck, and get a golf membership in a local country club. It was not—and I cannot stress this enough—that I'd get a degree that would have me share an elevator and maybe a cafeteria with people with white coats, stethoscopes, and proficient golf swings. A job in a health field was no substitute for becoming a doctor.

---

6 This, according to my husband, was the first thing I told him when we met two weeks after I arrived. I don't remember it but I'm going to take his word for it mainly because I'd just spent eight months in immigration in Italy, the birthplace of Ferrari, and also because *everyone* in the Soviet Union knew that American streets were paved with gold and what is a $300,000 car when that's the case? PS: Now I know that Ferraris are overrated because you cannot drive one at the speeds that God and the engineers intended when you have unbribable police in your wake.

Honestly, I'm not sure why I thought it was. Possibly because I was young but also maybe because I was desperate for their approval. Which, of course, never came and that's how I learned that compromises are overrated. NO ONE won. I ended up paying a gazillion dollars for a degree that's basically just a wall decoration I cannot read,[7] my parents still have blank expressions when asked about what I studied (and why I studied it in the first place since I barely worked in the field!), and avoiding non-weather related conversations like it was a Komsomol parade hell has pretty much become a given.

But back to the much more recent past and why my mother was upset with me. I couldn't imagine which part of our last weather conversation had angered her, and so being a mature adult and not someone who still feels like a teenager when conversing with her parents, I inquired as to what was wrong. Coaxing it out of her took some effort because my mother grew up in the Soviet Union and is pretty much still in agreement with the Communist Party about hard labor. When she finally replied, she said she felt hurt that her granddaughter—my daughter—didn't share anything personal with her. And that it was all my fault. Which wasn't really that unusual because most of my daughter's shortcomings have historically been my fault.

Still, to be open-minded (and also logical) I started to point out that her granddaughter was a junior in college and that whatever sharing she was doing was basically her own decision because I didn't have that kind of sway over a 20-year-old. I also planned to explain that maybe there were things my mother didn't want to know and that non-knowing had this special charm about it that allowed you

---

7 It's in Latin! WHY?

to actually sleep at night. Finally, I was also going to mention that my daughter didn't share everything with me either, which I thought would make my mother feel good because she could be competitive. But I didn't get to do any of the above because she interrupted me and said it was all my fault because I didn't *properly* explain to my daughter how jinxing worked.

Say what?

That was so unfair. Mainly because I think of myself as a mother who's been very good at imparting crucial life lessons but also because I know exactly how jinxing works. I was there in the Soviet Union where this highly intricate and extremely effective system hung over the populace in a grey cloud thicker than Brezhnev's eyebrows and heavier than Putin's kompromat file on Trump. Plus I was pretty confident that my explanation touched on all the important things my child needed to know. The rules were pretty straightforward: anyone who envied you could jinx you—except blue-eyed people. Like, for example, when I told a brown-eyed girl that my father brought me a pair of jeans from his trip to East Berlin, she must have jinxed me because the next thing I knew he was demoted off foreign travel by order of someone at the KGB who didn't take lightly to his refusal to join their informer ranks, and I never got jeans again. It's possible that if that friend didn't jinx me, the KGB wouldn't have been interested in my father. So basically, to avoid being jinxed stay mum about anything and everything good that either happened or may happen in your life—unless you're talking to a blue-eyed person. You see how this works?

Anyway, these days I rarely think about jinxing, but my daughter brought it up because somehow she became convinced that I jinx all of her relationships.[8] Explaining this crucial blue-eyed exception meant I could *never* be a jinxer and she could tell me everything. (It also meant I wasn't able to jinx anyone when I was growing up and that really sucked because it could have been helpful as a revenge against that girl but also against that fifth-grade boy who pushed me into the snow every time he walked past.)

Turned out I forgot about two things when I was explaining the jinxing:

1) That my mother has brown eyes.
2) That my daughter is very smart and will now use that fact as an excuse to keep her grandmother from knowing more than she wants her to know.

Which is why my mother sounded icy and distant and was also schooling me in jinxing rules, and especially the one that stipulates that A FAMILY MEMBER CAN *NEVER* JINX YOU[9] and how could I ever forget that? I nodded and apologized for such a grave mistake on my part and was about to wrap up the conversation and go back to watching a re-run of *The Good Place* on my phone when she skillfully segued into the unsafe topic of *my life*. She wondered if my confusion about jinxing rules led me to never share anything

---

8 Something about them ending *right after* she told me about them. You see how crucial it was for me to teach her the rules?

9 Honestly, I'm not entirely sure it's a real rule because you could have some pretty awful family members, in which case you definitely need to worry about them jinxing you but also maybe about other things.

either and now that we had it all cleared away I could start sharing. I was about to lie and say that my battery was at one percent, but then something possessed me and I acted like a mature person and instead answered that jinxing had nothing to do with me not sharing. Which I immediately regretted because it led to more questions, a very long phone call, and no time to either watch *The Good Place* or do a Google search to see if I could immediately enroll in a Trump University course on effective lying.

We spoke for over an hour. And I shared how I felt. Which was weird, but also strangely wonderful—not only because I didn't have to look for more ingenious ways to make weather interesting but also because I had actual guts to tell my mother MY side of our-immigration-and-consequent-decision-making story. And I told it like the actual boss I've become in the last thirty-one years, one month, fourteen days, eight hours and twenty-one minutes since we left Moscow.

She listened *without* any judgment. Or without the sighs so many of us children of Soviet-Jewish émigrés know to interpret as extreme disappointment. Most likely because she felt relieved I never thought of her as a jinxer but also because the statute of her disappointment had probably expired. And also because in the last thirty-one years, one month, fourteen days, eight hours and twenty-one minutes she too has learned something about endocrinology.

STUBBORN AND (NOW) PROUD OF IT

I wish the phrase "nevertheless she persisted" existed 30 years ago when the guy who later became my father-in-law took to calling me "stubborn." If that had been the case, I would have purchased a T-shirt with this phrase printed on it so that I could passive-aggressively wear it every time I saw him. And a long-sleeve shirt. And a sweater. And a baseball hat—maybe even one for him too. Because, you know, you can't emphasize this point enough.

But, alas, if I were being honest, back then I wouldn't have had the guts. Or the confidence. Mainly because I was a fresh-off-the-boat Homo Sovieticus who believed that Americans knew *everything* better, but also because the American in question was older and respect for elders was embedded in me with the same force as the date of Lenin's birthday (if I ever get dementia, ask me when Lenin was born and it'll be the only date I'll remember). Where I came from, speaking your mind or disagreeing with older people—and especially older men—while inhabiting the body of a young woman was just as against the natural order of things as failing at piano when your entire family consisted of musical geniuses.

Which is to say that I'd like a time machine please, so I can go back and gift my younger immigrant self some badly needed guts.[1] And some insight into how a thesaurus works. Because then I would have pointed out that he could have called me tenacious or

---

1 And also a talent for music.

steadfast or determined, because *that's what we call a man who doesn't give up*. And that calling me stubborn made it sound like he was scolding me as if I was a child WHEREAS I was an adult who had just orchestrated an entire across-the-ocean-from-behind-the-Iron-Curtain-move that involved faking Soviet exit visas, smuggling an heirloom bracelet through Soviet customs, learning two languages, and also selling lacquer boxes and Red Army watches at midnight on the streets of Rimini (I have no idea why Red Army watches were in such demand in Italy). Would a child have been able to do that? Would *he* have been able to do that?

All of this is to say that being stubborn works. Older men in my life (read: my dad and, later, my father-in-law) may not have liked it, but it literally got me where I wanted to be. Namely:

- in the United States
- NOT in New York City.

Here's why.

THE NEW HAMPSHIRE STORY

Like any tragi-comedy, the New Hampshire story involved family relationships and commenced a decade prior to the event my parents came to refer to as the "blood-turns-out-to-be-thinner-than-water experience," I came to refer to as the "real-America-here-I-come episode," and my grandfather came to refer to as the "stop-argu-ing-it'll-all-be-fine-in-the-end lecture." He was wise this way, my *dedushka*. Mostly because he was older than all of us, but also because it was his side of the family that was at the root of the New Hampshire story. Namely his nephew, the nephew's wife, and the nephew's son (although to be fair, the son had very little to do with it because he was still too young to have any effect on his parents' decision; he was maybe 25, which in Soviet-Jewish families is like being seven for boys and five for girls).

Just to give you a bit of a background, my grandfather pretty much raised his nephew. That's because both of his parents died at a young age. His mother, my *dedushka*'s sister, died of breast cancer (that BRCA gene is nasty, I'm telling you) and his father ended up in a gulag, which was very sad but not at all unusual.[2] The nephew came to live with my grandparents and, because he was older and they were working ungodly-hour shifts to build that bright future Stalin promised after the war, he ended up babysitting my mother and basically raising her. All of this is to say that this nephew was the closest nephew my *dedushka* ever had.

Which is why when, in 1979, the nephew and his wife bailed out of the Soviet Union with the first wave of Jewish immigration, the nephew told my grandfather he'd be waiting for us with open arms and an open door. To entice us (and also to brag a little because bragging is a rite of passage for any Soviet immigrant), he and his family proceeded to send us photos of their lives in America as soon as they landed. Those photos mainly included them posing in front of huge

---

2 The nephew's father was a French communist who came to the Soviet Union to build a bright future but ended up being accused of espionage and named an "enemy of the people," which must have been very confusing for him because he was definitely *not* the enemy; the mustached creep in the Kremlin was.

houses and large cars which weren't theirs. But because the American dream consisted of buying *something* large, they were taking pictures of their dreams. Which was completely understandable and also, at times, infuriating.

Infuriating because my father wasn't the enticeable sort. It took almost ten years of Buicks and LA mansions to convince him that his future was probably brighter in California. When he finally did get convinced (by me *because I was stubborn and kept trying to talk him into it*), it was only after my grandfather checked in with his nephew if the offer of open arms still stood, and the nephew sent back an unequivocal "yes" along with a fake invitation designed to fool the Soviet authorities. To give you some background but not to make it too long, I will summarize the fake invitation business in a handy, almost bullet-points kind of format.

Reagan got Gorbachev to agree to let the Jews go.

But Gorbachev (together with the Politburo) had a few tricks up his sleeve and said that he'd only allow the Jews to reunite with family in their ancestral homeland. Which, according to the Communist Party, was Israel. Where *most* Soviet Jews didn't have *any* family. (A brilliant move by the Party, especially considering the fact that most of them had no strategic thinking whatsoever. It just goes to show you that, where screwing Jews was concerned, they definitely knew their game.)

Instead of going to Israel where they didn't know anyone, most Soviet Jews wanted to reunite with families *wherever* those families were. Which is understandable, because who wants to start their lives all over again, all by themselves in a new land when there are relatives who can help elsewhere? (Remember this point, it's *crucial*.)

So a few American Jewish organizations got really creative (take that, scheming Politburo!) and invented—Gogol's *Dead Souls* style—a bunch of non-existent Israeli relatives for every Soviet Jew who wanted to leave. And then they got even more creative and exploited the loophole that the Politburo had forgotten about: the Soviet Union didn't have a diplomatic relationship with Israel. There were *no* planes flying from Moscow to Tel Aviv and that meant everyone who declared they were going to Israel *had* to fly through a third country. In 1989, that was Vienna. Which is where the HIAS representative met you at the plane and asked you point blank if you were going to Israel.

To which 95 percent of Soviet Jews—including us—answered no.[3]

To summarize: we all got out using fake invitations that said we were going to reunite with aunt Rosa and uncle Moses in Israel, then flew to Vienna, disembarked, and declared we were going to America, Canada, or Australia.

Brilliant move, us.

Because all of the above wasn't entirely fail-proof (the Soviets could refuse you the exit visa and then you became a *refusenik*,[4] which in Russian basically meant a person with no future in the

---

3 Or at least 95% of our flight. Which might have been representative, but who am I to say? I'm not a statistician. But it does explain why my *How to Become a Westerner 101* course took place in Europe.

4 A Soviet citizen of Jewish origin who's been denied permission to emigrate. Also, one of the words the Soviet Union successfully contributed to the Merriam-Webster dictionary, which clearly made the USSR a superpower with lasting power and influence. Other words

USSR and in antisemite meant the scum of the Earth), my father was only prepared to risk it if the future on the other side of the Iron Curtain came with a cup of tea and good advice at a relative's house. Because the nephew's wife knew how to make a mean cup of tea and because by the time we would arrive the nephew would have had a good ten years' experience of living in the US and thus plenty of insider tips, my father agreed.

You've already read the details of our exodus in an earlier essay and know that we'd made it out of the Soviet Union, landed in Vienna, told the balding man we were going to America, and after three weeks in Austria were promptly shipped to Rome, where American authorities set up shop to interview every wannabe refugee from the Soviet Union. That interview was going to be the single most important interview of our lives because if you didn't pass it you wouldn't get refugee status and your life as you know it would be over. And by over I mean you wouldn't get to go to America, and you couldn't stay in Italy, and you couldn't return to the Soviet Union even if you wanted to because in the last ditch effort to teach the treacherous Jews a lesson, the Politburo stripped you of your citizenship when you left. All of this basically meant that if you didn't get that refugee status you'd be as good as Gogol's *Dead Souls* dead.

Which is why my father told me to shut up and not say a word during the interview. I was happy to oblige, but mainly because the people interviewing us looked like they'd stepped out of the latest Komsomol movie and were there to accuse us of sabotaging the

---

include *gulag*, *samizdat*, and *agitprop*. *Kompromat* will probably be next, if Putin has anything to say about it.

collective farm tractors. Unfortunately for him, one of them turned to me in the middle of the interview and asked me to recount a few instances of antisemitism that affected my daily life. This put me in the unfortunate situation of trying to figure out what he meant by "a few" (it could be three, five, fifteen; how was I *even* supposed to pass this test?) and deciding which out of several thousand antisemitic incidents to choose from—all while seeing my father cringe at the thought that I was going to ruin *everything*. Really, confidence in my storytelling abilities was never his strong suit.

If the interview was the closest definition I could cite for hell (we were Soviet atheists and up until that point, hell for us was standing in line for butter for three hours while being insulted about long noses or bulging eyes and *then* coming home without any butter), waiting three weeks for the result was in a different category of hell altogether. I'm guessing it was similar to what happens when hell contains not only the three Komsomol-look-alike interviewers but also all the butter you could ever want except that you can't get to it. And that's why I spent those three weeks eating a lot of pasta with butter, which was way cheaper than parmesan and available any day of the week without queuing.

At the end of three weeks my ability to tell a compelling story was rewarded and we got our refugee status (if we hadn't, it would have been my fault.) We celebrated with more butter on pasta and I celebrated by basking in the glow of a *Slava bogu tiu nas ne provalila* compliment, which is Russian for "Thank God you didn't screw up" and my father's for "Well done on your part of it," and basically his highest compliment ever. But it turned out our celebrations were premature, and this is where my stubborn gene gets to shine again and where the New Hampshire story has its climax.

Well, almost.

Every refugee status came wrapped in the expectation that the relatives who sent you that fake invitation and who volunteered to be your sponsor would now make good on their promise and sponsor you. This didn't mean give you money or even help you with rent, but welcome you with open arms and an open door—basically what my grandfather's nephew was saying he would do when he sent us photos of Buicks and LA mansions. And what my father cited as one of the most important reasons he agreed to immigrate (the other one was that he was tired of my *stubbornly* begging him to agree).

But when we called my grandfather's nephew from a payphone in Italy and informed him that we were the proud new holders of the refugee status and were ready to come to join him in California to dream together about large cars and huge houses, he told us he was sorry. His exact words were "*U nas izmenilas obstoyatel'stva*," which meant "our situation has changed" and which we heard and understood as "someone you loved and trusted has just totally betrayed you and left you out in the cold on a street you've never been on." My father heard it as the biggest *fuck you* of his life and as the final straw of the evidence that no one on my mother's side of the family could be trusted.

Which brings us to the moment that went down in history as only the second debate I ever won with my father.[5] That happened between him snapping at my mother and my *dedushka* that it was all their family's fault and insisting that our only choice now was to go

---

5 The first one was convincing him to emigrate, in case you're reading this book in reverse.

MARGARITA GOKUN SILVER

to New York City. I took issue with him saying it was our *only* choice, because family-abandoned refugees like us had another choice and that was to wait for a smaller Jewish community anywhere else in the US to sponsor us. He wasn't thrilled with me pointing out the discrepancy with what he was saying[6] but he was even less thrilled with what *not* going to New York City might mean.

FATHER: We cannot wait because if we wait too long it'll be even harder to find jobs. I'm already 43 and your mother is 41.

ME [desperately searching my brain for names in case he asked for evidence]: Some people only wait two or three months.

FATHER: To go to New York, the wait is two weeks.

ME: But in New York we will never become American! We will never learn English or live among the Americans. (I must point out here that when we said New York we meant the Brighton Beach area of Brooklyn, where everyone going to New York was sent. Also known as Little Odessa. Also known as the section of the United States that was exactly like the Motherland, minus the Politburo, plus the Russian-mafia-enforced-capitalism. Also known as the place where your American dreams went to die.)

FATHER: We can move later.

ME [hyperventilating]: People don't! I'm not going to New York. No way.

In Moscow, whenever I had an argument with my father it always devolved into a lot of screaming and, in his case, a lot of saliva flying

---

6 Because my father was always right and because he was older I was never supposed to challenge him. I think I must have forgotten that rule or maybe the freedom was already playing with my head—I was in the West after all.

out of his mouth. In my case, it devolved into slamming our front door, telling them I was running away, and then hiding behind the trash chute of our building (my mother was smart and from a very young age indoctrinated me with threats of serial killers and rapists roaming the streets of Moscow; I was a wimp). In Italy, we had no trash chute and also running away would have defeated the purpose, because he would have used my absence to ignore my pleas and agree to go to New York.

Which is why I stayed. And I argued. And in the end, I won. *Because I was stubborn.* (And also because my grandfather helped me by taking my side and because he was older my father had to take his opinion into account. He was raised to respect elders. He wasn't a brute.)

FATHER: Fine. But we better not wait longer than two months.

We waited five. And when the news finally arrived that a community in New Hampshire wanted to sponsor us, we turned to each other and asked, "What is New Hampshire?" Then, because I felt responsible and because there was no internet yet, I volunteered to look it up at the local library, which was located very close to the beach and made for a good excuse to get out of the house while my father lamented agreeing to *my* stupid idea of not going to New York. Unfortunately, the town in which we lived was tiny and the only information about New Hampshire was an article with a photo of someone with a nose ring. I don't remember what the article said, but I remember that photo. Mostly because it made my father collapse into a chair and loudly moan, "*Gospodi*, where are we going?" and also look at me like as if I represented some great personal disappointment. Which I was used to, but this time it was confusing because it wasn't even *my* nose ring.

Long story short, that's how we ended up in New Hampshire. Which directly led to the following:

- My parents learning to speak English faster than they would have in Brighton Beach, which in turn allowed my father to find a professional job within weeks of arrival, thus sending him and my mother to another state and granting me the independence I had dreamt about ever since we started the whole immigration process in Moscow.

- My *dedushka* trying to learn English and not succeeding and thus deciding to reconcile with his nephew and move to Los Angeles where he could speak Russian for the rest of his life and also have easy access to *pelmeni*. This was a win for him but also for me because I was left completely alone with no adults trying to tell me what to do.

- Me meeting my future husband and making him listen to Soviet rock music which 100 percent contributed to us falling in love, because how could I resist a young man who praised one of my favorite bands without understanding a word of what they were singing? He also bought a Russian-language textbook with stickers that defined table as *stol* and chair as *stul* and dog as *sobaka*, and plastered them all over his house. The dog was *not* impressed. (Actually, now that I think about it, maybe my future father-in-law had some kind of inkling that I would marry his son and shaming me with that "stubborn" label was his attempt at avoiding having his house stickered forever and the dog traumatized.)

When my friend read this essay, she was like, "Why did your future father-in-law call you stubborn, what did you do?" and then I spent a very long time trying to remember and in the end my memory failed me. Which I realize undermines my argument but, hello, I'm not in court and it was a long time ago and the moral of the story here isn't that I refused to eat English muffins (because what are they even—failed bagels married to some kind of sponge?) and my future father-in-law loved serving them for breakfast whenever we were at his place. The moral of the story is that when you're a young immigrant, you don't always know how to reply and so you obsess over it for years and then you decide that the best way to right the wrong is to pen 3,000+ words on the subject and to have strangers read them and judge you for being a complete push-over. Which I've now done.

Because I'm stubborn like that.

DO YOU NEED *BLAT* TO GET INTO THE IVY LEAGUE OR WILL HAVING THE HISTORY OF THE COMMUNIST PARTY ON YOUR TRANSCRIPT SUFFICE?

When you immigrate to the US from behind the Iron Curtain, you ponder a lot of questions about America. Why are there no fences around these houses? I can see straight into their living room—don't they have curtains in this country? Cereal served with *cold* milk—what kind of soggy hell is that? This tomato has no taste—did it even come from the earth? Why do they call this game "football" if they carry the ball instead of kick it? What is tuition? HOW MUCH?

My US college experience began when I heard the answer to this last question and immediately wondered how I could bargain it down. Even with a grant, a loan, and a scholarship, the final bill had more zeroes in it than there were medals on Brezhnev's chest, post the chest-expansion surgery.[1] Paying that amount for the next four years would attach more debt to my credit than my parents and grandparents had made in Soviet salaries during their entire careers—and, also, what was credit and how did debt work? So,

---

1 Not his real chest—his portrait's chest. They ran out of space for painting in additional medals.

when someone suggested trying to transfer my grades from my Moscow university, I embraced the idea with the zeal of a former *zampolit*—a political education commissar in the Soviet army and, in my case, a role I was once assigned at age 13 during our school's re-enactment of the Battle of Stalingrad. (I poured my heart and soul into that role, mainly because it made me one of the bosses, but also because it didn't involve storming hills right after a heavy snowstorm.)

Once it was translated, I took my Moscow Oil and Gas Institute transcript to the liberal arts college where I was about to major in biology. The dean looked at the names of the courses I'd studied—drafting and thermodynamics and calculus and physics—and told me the best they could do was apply all of my calculus classes towards the math and science requirements. He then squinted at the transcript again and continued, "And maybe this one for your social science requirement." He pointed to the History of the Communist Party—a required course for any Soviet degree—which immediately made me ponder two things: (1) could this be the first time in the history of humanity that communism helped anyone lower their capitalist tuition, and (2), if so, would it be appropriate to send an entry to the *Guinness Book of World Records*?

Communism education shaving zeroes off my bachelor's degree cost wasn't the only surprise in store for me as I embarked on that illustrious higher education endeavor otherwise known as one of the backbones of the US debt industry. Here are a few more insights I learned along the way.

MY CLASSMATES DIDN'T CHEAT

I'd never taken or passed an exam in Moscow without cheating.[2] No one has—we all spent more time on coming up with ingenious ways to hide our crib notes than on studying. Mainly because popular wisdom claimed that *na rabote zabudesh' vse chto uchil v institute*, which basically meant that once we finished our degrees we wouldn't use anything we learned, but also because who could even understand those thermodynamics formulae? Certainly not those of us who never intended to be engineers and only went to study the subject because (1) the competition to get in was less fierce than in other places; (2) someone in our family knew someone on the admissions committee and in those days it didn't matter what degree you got as long as you got one; and (3) you were a person of Jewish origin and predestined to study engineering by your birthright in the USSR, also known as institutionalized antisemitism.

As a contrast, here's how my first midterm in the US went:

- The professor passed around the exam papers.
- He then left the classroom for the entire duration of the midterm.
- NO ONE produced any crib notes.
- NO ONE opened a textbook.
- NO ONE asked anyone for help.
- Everyone just sat there and *honestly* wrote what they knew.

---

2 It's been over 30 years so I'm going to go ahead and assume that whatever statute of limitations exists on those things has already passed.

- And so did I (once I recovered from the shock of "what the hell is wrong with these people?" and decided it was probably not a good idea to check those notes I'd made *just in case*).

Luckily I had studied for that exam. Which was already an improvement from my past Soviet student life and a good habit to have in this brave, new world of actually learning shit. Later, when I mentioned to a classmate of how stunned I was to see no one cheat, she looked at me with a weird look in her eye and said, "That's normal. You'd get expelled if you got caught." I wanted to mention that getting caught was probably unlikely with the professor being completely MIA but then decided against it because it's always important to make a good first impression. And then—because complete assimilation was my ultimate goal—I went on to finish my bachelor's and my master's without cheating even once. Which, if you think about it, was a huge personal win, because I haven't used anything I studied since I finished those degrees.

NO ONE CARES WHERE YOU'RE FROM

The first thing I did when I walked into my very first class was to approach the only other student who was there and introduce myself thusly: "Hello, I'm Margarita and I'm from the Soviet Union." Here's how I hoped the rest of the conversation would go:

THE OTHER STUDENT: Wow, tell me more about it!

Cue a long, involved chat about life under communism, about my journey to America, and how no, there were definitely no bears walking the streets of Moscow on their own.

Here's how it went instead:

THE OTHER STUDENT: Hi, I'm (name I don't remember).

Silence.

She didn't ask me any questions and calmly went back to leafing through the opened microbiology tome in front of her. Which seemed strange to me for two reasons: (1) I was from the USSR, a.k.a. the Evil Empire, a.k.a. the reason her neighbors probably had a dilapidated nuclear fallout shelter in their backyard; and (2) was microbiology really more fascinating than a real, incarnate foreigner standing in front of her?

Listen, it might sound strange to your ears but back then for me any foreigner was like a specialty store reserved only for Politburo members. I grew up behind the Iron Curtain, which never rose to allow us out but was occasionally lifted to let a few selected foreigners in. Whenever that happened, we ran to places where those foreigners were allowed to congregate—for example, a *Klub Internatsionalnoi Druzhby*, which (you guessed it) translated as Club of International Friendship, at a local Palace of Pioneers—and spent the evening in proper formation at the other end of the hall ogling said foreigners. Asking them questions or engaging with them was reserved for the chosen few, otherwise known as friends of the Palace director, but if you had a good viewing spot it was almost worth it because then you'd have something to imagine as you re-designed your mother's old skirt into the kind of skirt that girl from East Germany was wearing. And when you were finally allowed to converse with a foreigner—if you could call it conversing because at that point you could barely move your frozen lips after standing guard at a World War II monument in sub-zero temperatures for hours—you asked as many questions as their KGB overseers would allow without shooting you first.

Which is why my classmate's complete indifference was so shocking that I remained standing near her for an entire minute. And then, as if that wasn't embarrassing enough (because, trust me, she knew I was still standing there since she had no smartphone to disappear into), I actually took the vacant seat at her desk when the rest of the classroom was *completely* empty and I could have sat anywhere. Breaking, I'm sure, some kind of unspoken rule about how you're supposed to behave with strangers but, hey, I didn't grow up with the Berenstain Bears so what did I know? Plus, I was still hoping she'd ask me something and we'd have a complex conversation and form a beautiful friendship and now you know the extent of all of my Soviet dreams and how they didn't come true.

THEY DON'T PAY YOU—YOU PAY THEM

In the USSR, we made money just by going to a university. Sure, it wasn't a lot—50 roubles a month in my case—but it came in handy when I had to flag down a Soviet equivalent of an Uber[3] to get to school if I was running late or if a Komsomol chapter leader came to our classroom to collect monthly dues before I managed to escape. So imagine my surprise when I showed up for classes in the US after paying that ginormous tuition bill and was told that stipends weren't a thing. And that if I wanted my school to pay me

---

3 More proof that all of the current American conveniences were invented in the USSR.

any money I had to get a work-study job, which was another form of financial aid because every dollar I'd make there would go directly into my tuition payment and not towards that Pizza Hut special I'd been eyeing.

For two-and-a-half years I worked in what was then called a language lab and what's now called Rosetta Stone. Students came in to sign out cassettes of the language they were studying, sat behind a partition and stared blankly into space while mouthing words I hoped belonged to those languages and not to a rough draft of a future Unabomber manifesto. My responsibilities were to check the cassettes coming in and going out, and to keep the tape closet organized, neat, and fully stocked, all of which usually took about two minutes thirty-five seconds, so I spent the rest of my shift either attempting to study for that midterm during which I wasn't going to cheat or wondering if there was such a thing as boredom-induced brain atrophy. On the plus side, when I got my first paycheck I immediately cashed whatever remained of it after paying tuition and, because there were no Komsomol dues, I supersized my McDonald's meal that day and it almost felt like there was a stipend in my pocket.

"YOU DON'T NEED *BLAT* TO GET INTO YALE"

That's what my husband-to-be said when he encouraged me to apply to Yale. (If you're impressed with his knowledge of Soviet colloquialisms, I'll take that as a compliment.) And so, with the unwavering belief of a former Soviet in America as the Ultimate Land of Opportunity, I forked out the fee that could have paid for several Pizza Hut specials and sent in my application. Their program checked all the boxes: (1) it was health related and thus (I hoped) parent-approved; and (2) it was international and thus (definitely) my aspirations-approved. The fact that it came with an Ivy League degree was the cherry on the cake or, if you want a Soviet equivalent, a set of functioning windshield wipers in your Zhiguli.

Several weeks later I received a thick envelope, which meant my husband-to-be was right—you didn't need *blat* to get into Yale. What you *did* need was to be the very first former Soviet who applied less than a year after the collapse of the Soviet Union to a graduate course with the word "international" in its name. I'm not saying that's the *only* reason they accepted me, but I am saying it probably helped. Because whatever you required back then to be accepted into ranks almost as exclusive as the Kremlin burial wall—a WASP pedigree, a library wing named after your family,[4] that coy yet mysterious answer "Boston" when asked where they did their undergrad—I didn't have. All I had was a 3.8 GPA, a former zip code that was still probably nuclear warhead target #1 with the code name "Gorbachev's birthmark" or something less imaginative like "Commie, this one's for you," and a personal statement that somehow convinced the admissions committee that I knew exactly what I was doing applying to study public health when I had no clue what that even was.[5]

---

4 Otherwise known among the former Soviets as the homegrown, American version of *blat* (but not known as such among Americans, probably because it never made it into the Merriam-Webster).

5 Can they take my degree away if I admit this?

My two years at Yale were spent alternately trying to figure out how to make statistics palatable and how to persuade everyone around me, and especially snooty undergrads with their daddy's bank accounts, that those shoes I bought at Marshalls came from Neiman Marcus, weren't on sale, and didn't give me blisters. Trying to fit into the crowd of cool classmates who not only seemed to deeply care about the subject we were collectively spearheading— the International Public Health course was in its first year—but also understood the meaning of words like "community health agency" was hard. In Moscow, we just had state polyclinics to which we all went to get healed by doctors who, without any shiny toys, managed to diagnose what was wrong with us, prescribed antibiotics or whatever pill was needed at the time, and sent us home to convalesce, ALL courtesy of the state. *Why couldn't the US do this?* was basically the question I wanted to ask but never did, because *not* asking questions was how I avoided coming across as a nincompoop and, if you were ever an immigrant, you'd know how important that was.

COLLEGE SPORTS AS A THING

Okay, full disclosure—I'm not a sports person. I might have pretended to like Spartak, one of Moscow's football (oops, soccer!) teams, when I was a teen in the USSR, but you had to pick a team and Spartak seemed the coolest. So when in the US I finally got to grad school in a university large enough to have teams, I was perplexed. First of all, why does a university have to have a sports team unless it's the kind of university that grooms Olympic athletes? Second of all, who cares? And third of all, why do they care?

I just don't get this whole infatuation with college sports. I wouldn't be caught dead saying "GO [insert name of your university's team]" on my Facebook wall or aloud, or even if you paid me a stipend. Maybe that's because it's usually said in reference to football, which I still don't understand, or maybe it's because I don't get the intimate connection between academia and a sport that could literally damage your brain, or maybe it's because four hours is way too much of my lifetime to invest in watching huge guys in tights push and fight each other and call it a touchdown. (Do they? Do they call it a touchdown? I mean, I don't even know what a touchdown is so maybe I'm wrong and you're free to ignore me.)

When I was at Yale, the Harvard-Yale game was all the rage and I didn't even go once. Which clearly made me weird and uncool and probably not a team player, but I was in debt and tickets cost money and I would have much rather spent it on a cat tower for a kitten I'd rescued. Many of my classmates went and that's probably why we never kept in touch after we graduated, because sports fostered close connections and that was something I didn't understand, since back in the Soviet university stratosphere our connections were fostered by a shared lack of freedom, and infatuation with the Levi's none of us owned. It's something I still don't understand, and also—why 15 minutes in football are never the *actual* 15 minutes and are more like 15 hours?

It's been almost three decades since I graduated and two decades since I sent in my last student loan payment. Out of those decades I have worked in the field I was educated in for exactly three years, eleven months, and five days. Does it mean that all those hours I studied for midterms during which I didn't cheat and all that money I paid that ultimately went to finance some banker's second yacht were a complete waste? Yes and no. Yes, because it was a waste for reasons you've already read about in the *Great Expectations, the Beginning* essay and will read some more about in the *Should-Have-Done-It Bucket List* essay. And no, because it wasn't a *complete* waste. I have two degrees to hang on my wall (my very own equivalent of a Picasso investment), I get to practice being coy while saying I went to graduate school in New Haven, Connecticut, and I now know that if you're going to spend Sotheby's idea of a first bid on a degree, you better study what you want. Which is what I'm doing now, as I'm paying the tuition bill for my second master's.[6]

---

6 At another Ivy League. Kind of. See the *Should-Have-Done-It Bucket List* essay for details.

SEX AND THE SOVIET UNION

Do you remember that distracted boyfriend meme that just wouldn't die? The one where a guy walking down the street with his girlfriend turns to stare at the backside of a woman in a red dress while puckering his lips like he is at a construction site and the only thing keeping him from being encased in cement by his buddies is to be offensive? (Because obviously that's the only reason why catcalls are still a thing, right?) You've probably seen your share of this meme on Twitter or Facebook or Instagram and it's been used for anything from claiming socialism was better than capitalism (because socialism looks better in red) to making fun of em dashes (I feel like that was a dig in my direction, honestly, because em dashes are my favorite), to shaming millennials for loving their avocado toasts. (Sign me up! Not for the shaming, obviously. For the avocado toast.)

If I were to adapt this meme to this essay, the guy would be me, the girl in the red dress—men at airports, and the annoyed girlfriend in the blue top—no one (see how I just used the em dash there? Twice!). No one, because I'm discreet when I check men out at airports. Which basically means I don't pucker my lips and look like I'm about to digest them whole, Prada loafers included. The reason I don't pucker my lips is because I had Bell's palsy when I was 18 and my puckering isn't symmetrical. Which doesn't only *not* look cute but it also looks as if my dog just shit all over the bathtub and I'm skewing my mouth into a grimace to avoid swearing. (The Bell's palsy also made my eyebrows decide they don't need to be aligned and can pretty much travel around my forehead however they please, and it turned one of my eyes into a watering hole that springs tears out of nowhere like those fun fountains you run through when you want to get wet. All of this is to say that now you know all of my face deficiencies, so if you recognize me on the street and see one of my eyes leaking, please don't stare. And for the love of God, don't ask me what's wrong.)

But back to airport browsing. I've been married to my husband for over two decades and I still check men out at airports. It's possible I'm doing this because I've been married to him for so long, but don't tell him that. When I follow a semi-attractive man with my eyes, I don't do it because I lust after strangers, or because I'm looking for a fling, or because I like what they are wearing (although that's *one more piece of incriminating evidence* that my husband cannot dress to save his soul). I check these men out because I'm curious as to what it might have been like to have played the field a little more before going for that "death do us part," the Jewish version.

This will probably come as no surprise if you know anything about the Soviet Union, but all of this is happening to me because "there's no sex in the USSR." If you don't know much about the Soviet Union, let me catch you up on this significant part of its history:

- Gorbachev comes to power and announces *glasnost*, which basically stands for "you can now talk about whatever the hell you want, people."
- People begin to talk about gulags, about empty shelves in stores, and about whether Jews are to blame for everything—

gulags, empty shelves, and that birthmark on Gorbachev's forehead included.

- In an effort for the Iron Curtain to lift just a little bit or maybe to turn into one of those lacy curtains through which you can peek at your neighbor tuning his shortwave to *Voice of America*, Vladimir Pozner and Phil Donahue establish a series of bridges between the US and the USSR. In these what they call "Space Bridges," the Soviet TV audience can sit and gawk at all the Levi's in attendance on the other side, and the American audience can sit and wonder what the hell is wrong with Soviets and why they never smile.

- During one of those bridges, the conversation turns to sex in advertising, and a woman in the Soviet audience says, "There's no sex in the USSR and we're definitely against it." Someone yells out to point out she means *in advertising*, but that correction gets lost in either laughter or in consequent editing or in the abyss the Soviet Union is about to sink into, and the phrase goes down in history as "there's no sex in the USSR."

- Everyone in the US finds it hilarious but still wonders how the hell, if there's no sex in the USSR, are they populating all of those labor camps and why are the lines for butter so long?

My mother was *not* the woman in the audience, yet her attitude to sex could only be described as dating back to times when Anastasia was a real—not an animated—princess. For my mother, discussing sex with teenage me was paramount to cutting in line to buy toilet paper and having your ass handed to you in such a spectacular manner by the waiting *babushkas* that *pozor*[1] followed you long after you'd used it and gone back to the old issues of *Pravda*. She believed that just mentioning the word would cause me to have so much sex that I'd shame not only her, my father, both sets of my grandparents, my uncles, aunts, cousins, and far-removed relatives somewhere on the Kamchatka Peninsula, but also our ancestors all the way back to the times of the First Temple.

Shame and sex were tightly intertwined in the Soviet Union— only when it came to girls, naturally. Years later, comparing notes on coming of age in Moscow with my contemporaries who came of age in Western Europe and the US, I learned that there was that same shame-sex connection, only it happened *in their mother's generation*. The Soviet Union was usually behind on most things[2] so it's not surprising that our sexual revolution was a few decades late.

My mother's position on sex was singular—*just don't do it*. Until you're married, that is. She preached this with the same fervor Bolsheviks used to preach the opposite in the first few years after the Revolution. She also sniffed me every time I came home from a party, convinced that girls who smoked and drank were one ash flick away from intercourse, two from *frequent* sex, and three from being *easy*.

According to her, girls who smoked were on their way to a slut-hood so devastating no one would ever love them. Or invite them

---

1 Shame x1,000,000,000,000,000,000,000,000.

2 Except, of course, for being the first in space. And, generally, in ice-skating. And in gymnastics. And, possibly, in chess. And, according to the Politburo, in nuclear warheads. Although they may have been lying—none of us ever got to check.

on a date to a Red Army choir concert, bring them a bouquet of carnations (the Soviet flowers of choice for teenage dating), and then chastely walk them home. Girls who smoked would never be married and they would never become respected members of society. Nor would they then raise girls who also only had sex after marriage (or boys who didn't marry girls who smoked or had sex before marriage), and become the kind of mothers who sniffed their daughters for nicotine-infused sexual indiscretion.

AND I BELIEVED HER.

When I look back at my teenage years, I take my hat off to my mother. Her brainwashing techniques were far superior to those of the Politburo, because she actually got me to believe that *sex was bad*. I distinctly remember speaking to a boy who liked some girl in our class—a girl who'd had a few boyfriends—when he asked me if he should try approaching her.

"Don't do it," I said, shaking my head as vigorously as if I'd just heard of his plans to join the Red Army earlier than his draft date. "She'll do something very bad to you."

"What is it?" he asked, genuinely bewildered. "She'll break it off with me and I'll get hurt?"

Let me pause here and allow the fact that I *was* 16 to sink in. And still I had no idea that, as far as those boys were concerned, those "bad things" weren't bad at all (I blame the absence of internet). Even worse, I *really* believed boys wanted some old-time, tear-jerky romance where they courted girls for years, then got drafted into the Red Army and treasured their girlfriends' letters, and then came back and proposed. And then the couple lived happily ever after, raising perfect Soviet children and singing "The Internationale."

Thank God I had enough sense *not* to spell it out for him. Apparently I wasn't stupid, just brainwashed. So I nodded—the words "hurt" and "bad things" could generally go together so technically it was true—and said, "Yes, that's it. That's *exactly* what she's going to do."

He never approached that girl. Today I wonder if I had prevented a relationship that would have produced a child who could have taken down Putin and made the world great again. Instead, we got MAGA and it is possibly all my fault.

Since I didn't want anyone to think of me as a slut, I didn't smoke[3] or drink vodka.[4] Still, being liked by boys was something I aced as a young teen; the rumor in school was that even the most antisemitic of boys—the one who never lost an opportunity to call me *zhidovka*—was secretly in love with me. Boys fought for the right to carry my backpack to and from school and once a boy actually asked me out on a date—a classic let's-go-see-the-Red-Army-choir-and-here-is-a-bouquet-of-carnations kind of date. My mother was elated, but I broke up with him almost right after that concert. Not because I didn't enjoy the Red Army choir—who doesn't love a rendition of "Guard" sung by pot-bellied men in uniforms reminiscent of Stalin's secret police?—but because I was growing up and becoming interested in bad boys. And one bad boy in particular.

---

3 Here I should probably thank my mother for turning me off cigarettes and, potentially, preventing lung cancer.

4 Although to be honest that was mostly because vodka was gross and I never got used to the feeling of the complete annihilation of your throat when you downed a shot.

If you're thinking my story is about to follow an old, tired trope in which a good girl dates a bad boy while hoping to turn him into a decent member of society, you're wrong. That's *not* what happened in my case. Mostly because by the time I was 15 I could not have cared less about turning anyone into a Soviet specimen who could recite the Komsomol bylaws by heart while shooting a Kalashnikov engraved with the words "The Communist Party will lead us to victory," but also because we didn't actually date. Since I really liked him and since my mother was in my head *a lot*, and according to her ignoring boys would get them to fall in love with you forever, I spent the next two years doing just that while catching the occasional glance he threw in my direction and convincing myself that my plan was working. Even though he kept dating other girls.

By the time we graduated from high school we hadn't said more than two words to each other. The night of the prom I sent him telepathic messages to invite me to the dance, but he ignored them. When dawn broke over Moscow, I walked home barefoot—and alone—quietly berating myself for listening to my mother (and also swearing aloud at the guy who'd charged my grandfather money plus a bribe of caviar for the pair of foreign shoes that had given me blisters). But in the best example of when *zakon podlosti*[5] actually works to your advantage and things happen when you least expect them, I woke up to a phone call from him. Inviting me on a date.

Here are my thoughts in the exact order in which they appeared in my head when he asked me to go to the movies with him:

---

5 Translates as the equivalent of Murphy's Law but with a lot more comeuppance.

OMG, he is in love with me.
OMG, what should I do?
OMG, why does my voice sound so squeaky?
OMG, what am I going to wear?
OMG, my mother's plan ACTUALLY worked.

But the relationship didn't last. Mainly because we were going off to different universities and mine involved being shipped off to harvest potato fields for the entire month of September. This happened because students were cheap labor (read: free) and farm collectivization wasn't quite working out as well as the Politburo wanted the West to believe. Also, housing hormone-raging youth together in tiny construction huts was a Soviet government plan for fomenting new family units brought together by shared passion for hard, honest labor and a complete lack of heating. Being away from home on my own for the first time ever gave me the freedom to not be sniffed by my mother after each party and I promptly used it to make out in dark corners with a guy whose name was Valera or Kostya or Ivan or Sergei (who can remember?). I mainly did it to keep warm but also because he played the guitar during the nightly campfire.[6]

When I came back to town, I wasn't planning on telling my two-year crush about Valera, but apparently Moscow is a village and he already knew. We broke up, not because of my infidelity and because I denied everything, but because he was convinced I'd never love him. I had become so good at pretending to ignore him and acting

---

6 We used the campfire to roast stolen potatoes. Maybe that's why whatever we harvested never really made any difference to the collective farms.

as if he still had to win me over that he thought I didn't like him at all. Whereas I was madly in love with him. Which makes me a great actress, by the way. But also a complete idiot.

After that my love life was practically non-existent until I moved to America.[7] That was for two reasons: (1) in the USSR you dated at 18 or 19 or 20 *not* to have fun, but to find yourself a husband—no one wanted to be an old maid and old maidenhood began promptly on your 23rd birthday; and (2) husband-hunting was completely impractical because I had to marry a Jewish man and the young Jewish men I knew had either bad breath, or bad skin, or a pleading puppy look that comes with living in the provinces and studying in Moscow only because their mother wanted them to find a wife with a Moscow residency.

Marrying a non-Jew was out of the question because that was just as bad as sex before marriage. That was because there was *tol'ko odin shag ot liubvi k nenavisti*, which meant "only one step from love to hate" for any normal Soviet person and "your spouse will call you a *zhidovka* every time you fight" for a Soviet-Jewish person.

---

7 Unless you count a short liaison with a guy who called himself Mike instead of Mikhail, wore wide pants tucked into cowboy boots, and sported a cowboy hat that elicited asinine comments from the communist-leaning *babushkas*. He turned out to be 35, almost twice my age, and he didn't think walking me home late at night after a concert was necessary at all. Both of those things were basically a crime in my mother's dating handbook. Needless to say, I never mentioned either his age or his absence by my side as I navigated the dark streets of our neighborhood, hoping not to be murdered by the serial killers my mother always talked about.

Since being called *zhidovka* was basically my life at school and since, according to my parents, Moscow was full of Jews who married non-Jews and were now regretting it, I knew I wouldn't be able to bring home a Russian boy and survive it.

All of this is to say that when I moved to the US I was primed to marry the first Jewish boy who didn't have bad breath or bad skin. Which I did. Thus, foregoing all possible dating experience that seemed like a rite of passage for America's young and, in fact, is probably part of the Constitution. (If it isn't, it should replace the Second Amendment.) Don't get me wrong—my husband is great and there's no one I'd rather go to a Red Army concert with.[8] But my lack of diverse dating experiences is exactly what makes me follow a well-dressed man at an airport with my eyes and daydream just a little. It was also, incidentally, what made me order the *Girls and Sex* book for my daughter when she was 15 and embarrass her on more than 58 occasions by talking about everything. It's possible I've overdone it,[9] but I think this is a good thing because I don't want her to be browsing in airports when she's my age. Mostly because of that healthy relationship to sex I want her to have but also because it's probably not going to be easy because of all the plexiglass they've put up everywhere since Covid.

---

8 Remarkably, they're still a thing. I bet it's because Putin has plans to resurrect the Red Army like he's resurrected the absence of freedom of speech that the Soviet Union was so famous for.

9 Some say buying her a vibrator was a bit too much, but I disagree. Plus, I bought it when she was 16. I'm not a monster.

THE HUSBAND, PART 1, OR MY FIRST
(AND ONLY) AMERICAN ROMANCE STORY

My future husband's first impression of me was formed at a meeting he attended that was loosely titled "We are expecting this family of Russian Jews to land any moment now and what the hell are we going to do with them?" The meeting was held in Nashua, New Hampshire, circa May 1990 by a group of people from a local synagogue who had single-handedly saved my family from waiting in Italy until we all turned 90, or until my father disowned me for promising him a short wait but instead ending up in an immigration wait so long that he had to work as a driver for a Lubavitch Rabbi and teach him how to navigate a map in Rome. I have nothing but respect for my father for that. Driving into Rome while recently Soviet was a feat in and of itself. Driving in with a religious figure who didn't know his east from his west was an achievement worthy of a Hero of Socialist Labor medal.

Because my future father-in-law attended the same synagogue where the group that saved us from Italian oblivion was founded, he suggested that his son join them. At that time, Keith had just graduated from college and was hanging around doing nothing or, as he called it, "waiting for the Peace Corps to accept him" (or to assign him, who can remember?). And since we were refugees and he was interested in refugee affairs, he decided what the hell and attended the first meeting. Here's how that meeting went:[1]

---

1 Not exact quotes, obviously, because I wasn't there, but also because I usually tune out when my husband tells this story to people for the 759th time.

A COMMITTEE MEMBER: There's this young girl in the family who wants to continue her college education. But they have no money.

OTHER COMMITTEE MEMBERS [nodding and clearly thinking of the million dollar tuitions they'd paid themselves]

A COMMITTEE MEMBER: She'll need to work a few years to save. Maybe she can start by cleaning houses.

OTHER COMMITTEE MEMBERS [nodding and clearly thinking of dinner waiting for them at home because my fate was the last item on their agenda]: Good idea!

KEITH: Wait, what?

EVERYONE [looking at him]: And you are?

KEITH: I went through four years of college and I didn't have money when I started. That's what student loans are for.

OTHER COMMITTEE MEMBERS: What are student loans?[2]

OTHER COMMITTEE MEMBERS [nodding and still thinking of that dinner at home but now realizing this might take longer]: Hmmm.

A COMMITTEE MEMBER: I sit on the board of directors of the local liberal arts college. I can ask if they'd help.

OTHER COMMITTEE MEMBERS: That's perfect! Settled then. Young person who proposed this amazing idea we could never

---

2 Okay, maybe they didn't ask that. I just couldn't resist an opportunity to sound like Maggie Smith in *Downton Abbey* when she asked, "What is a weekend?" and the quote went down in history as her most badass ever and also as a piece of really tight writing I aspire to.

have thought of, will you explain the student loan situation to that young lady and generally take her under your wing?[3]

My first impression of my future husband was that he didn't have a nice car. That assessment was based on two things: (1) the hot minute I spent in the US before we met, and (2) the cars of two young men and one young woman who were also directed by their family members to take me under their wings and show me what it was like to be young in America. Which basically amounted to them driving me places while probably thinking, *I-am-so-bored-this-woman-has-no-idea-of-what-baseball-is-and-anyway-what-kind-of-weird-name-is-Margarita-isn't-it-a-drink-and-a-pizza?* and amounted to me thinking, *OMG-I'm-out-with-a-real-American-and-this-guy-is-fairly-cute-and-I-can-see-myself-dating-and-marrying-him-and-also-what-is-baseball?* Except there was one time when a girl took me over to her house and the van she drove had a car phone (WOW) and when I asked where one could call on that phone she smiled and said I could call the Soviet Union if I wanted, and I died.[4] And then I died again when we got to her house and they had an in-ground pool.

Clearly those other people didn't have any idea what taking someone under their wing meant because they never called or came back after that one time. Keith did, however. Which obviously worked in his favor in spite of his car, because I had no friends yet and

---

3 This is precisely why both my husband and his father now like to say that Keith "scooped me fresh from the boat," which I find wrong on so many levels, not the least of them that there was NO boat. We arrived by plane. Also there was no scooping of any kind involved ever.

4 Okay, fine, I've dated myself here.

spending 24/7 in a two-bedroom apartment with my parents and my grandfather had its limits. Plus, unlike those other people with convertible Saabs and car phones that could dial Gorbachev, Keith exhibited a fair amount of interest in my background and knew where Moscow was on the map and that it wasn't in Ohio. To my surprise this was light years away from most other young Americans who, when I introduced myself, asked, "Where is the Soviet Union?"[5]

Keith and I started out as friends and my first act of friendship was almost totaling his (not so nice) car as I maneuvered it out of the parking lot on my first driving practice for a license exam. He screamed "watch out" and I think this marked the moment when I lost all belief in my Soviet driving classes where I had spent the previous year learning to drive a Lada and also pretending to understand its combustion system. It also marked the moment when I melted just a little bit towards Keith, because who in his right mind would volunteer a car for an experiment that could end in an accident and also in an insurance premium increase? (Apparently not the guy with the convertible Saab who, by the way, was a lawyer which in English meant "someone who practices law" and in the recent-Soviet-émigré meant "a very very very very very rich person.") On the plus side, it turned out that in America you could drive an automatic, which meant I didn't have to coordinate my legs. (Hello, who could possibly press down with one foot while letting go with

5 See Footnote 2, but also I swear it felt as if they often had no clue where their country's former arch enemy number one was because their reaction to the fact that I'd recently arrived from the EVIL EMPIRE was a blank look.

another while AT THE SAME TIME trying to figure out where to turn in a town to which you've just moved and where all the signs are in another language and where the cops are ticket-happy because they have to finance their budgets in a state with no income or sales tax and where you're just trying to move this vehicle along without causing a major collision or a cacophony of horns? Answer: no one.)

After I didn't crash his car and actually got a license without having to bribe anyone at the DMV or bring a jar of caviar as an additional payment, Keith and I settled into the kind of friendship I called "he-is-a-nice-guy-but-I-am-going-to-try-finding-someone-with-a-nicer-car-for-dating-purposes." That thinking didn't last long because guys with nice cars were boring and also, in one case, drove me to their sister's new house where she had moved after getting married and left me downstairs with that sister[6] while making his way upstairs to retrieve a teddy bear which he proceeded to hug while lamenting that his sister had had to get married and move (I think I dodged a bullet there, don't you?).

Keith and I started dating three months into our friendship, which sticks out in my memory as the time when my parents packed their newly purchased, very-used Nissan Sentra and moved to Ohio for my father's new job. In Keith's memory, it sticks out as the moment when I was sad about my parents' departure and he tried to comfort me. Which I disagree with, because my parents moving

---

6 For a chat! We had *nothing* to chat about mainly because I still hadn't mastered the art of small talk Americans are so good at and she had no idea whether the Soviet Union was real or a setting for the Boris and Natasha cartoon.

away and leaving me on my own was my American dream, Phase 1, since it finally gave me the independence I should have had years ago, but also gave me my own bedroom in the two-bedroom apartment we had occupied since arrival. Until then, I'd had to share with my grandfather and he snored.

Our dating during those first weeks included:

- Him jumping out of my bedroom window—because he stayed the night and my *dedushka* still lived in the apartment—and then coming around to the front door as if he'd just driven up to the building. I feel like that was the most American adolescent experience I was ever going to have without being an actual adolescent or spending my adolescence in America.

- My *dedushka* calling him "Kisa," which was his way of pronouncing the unpronounceable "th" but also jokingly referring to a name Ostap Bender called his accomplice Ippolit Matveevich in the very famous *The Twelve Chairs* movie[7] every Soviet citizen has watched at least 286 times. I did *not* enjoy this reference because I was in the US to forget I was ever that Soviet citizen.

- Me eating supermarket French fries along with raw radishes, sliced and salted in the best tradition of Soviet healthy cuisine, and him staring at me and at the radishes and asking, "What

7 Based on the eponymous satirical novel by two Soviet writers Ilya Ilf and Evgeny Petrov, which spawned almost as many cinematic adaptations in the USSR and abroad as there were chairs in the book.

are those?" and then trying them and immediately spitting them out.

- Me receiving my first heating bill and virtually dying because it was more than the rent I had to pay for the apartment and because in the Soviet Union no one paid for heating because communist elves made sure it was always there and free. Him (and me) having to put on several sweaters and a coat to exit my room because after that bill, and after my *dedushka* moved to California, I only heated my bedroom so outside my door it felt like the Ice Age and tundra combined.

- Me meeting his friends and telling one of them that he was "too big to eat cake." I'm not proud of this.

- Me accidentally (or was it?) spraying perfume in his eyes two days before he was to leave for the Peace Corps. He took this as evidence of my great love and I took it as evidence that he shouldn't go, because then I'd be left behind and who knew where else I'd manage to spray that perfume? All I'm saying is that I didn't trust myself to see straight after he left, which, now that I think of it, could have been actual evidence of great love.

Another piece of evidence was that we spent the next two years of his Peace Corps experience writing snail mail letters to each other (there was no email yet and no WhatsApp! How did we survive?) and I also wrote letters to a friend of mine about how much I missed him (long distance was expensive). She later told me the letters made her cry, which I took as a compliment and a sign that I was going to be a great writer, which came in handy when I decided to drop endocrinology and never become a doctor.

Keith did his Peace Corps assignment in Panama and, on his second summer there, I went to visit him despite my parents' misgivings about me going alone on my first international trip (I was 23!) and also me leaving at the same time that my father's parents were visiting from Russia. That was summer 1992, several months after the collapse of the Soviet Union, and, in an effort to see first-hand what their son's life was like and whether he still thought it was worth abandoning the country that "fed and educated him,"[8] my *babushka*, along with my vehemently communist *dedushka*, braved acquiring a filthy-capitalist entrance visa to the former USSR's arch enemy number one, taking a train ride from their Black Sea town to Moscow during which they got robbed by bandits rehearsing their skills for the upcoming Wild-West-Russia-Edition of the 1990s, and living for a month in a small American town where no one spoke Russian, the TV was only in English, and the cold cuts tasted like cardboard. When they finally left to go back home, my *dedushka* declared this whole capitalist experiment a failure and asked my parents if he should put together a monthly care package for them.

---

8 The exact words my uncle uttered when, while still in the USSR and getting ready to emigrate, my parents had to ask for permission to leave from the immediate family members who weren't going. Which was basically my father's parents and his younger brother. My grandmother had no issues with it, my grandfather smoked several packs of cigarettes to calm his communist nerves and to help him decide whether he should disown my father at the same time as he signed that permission, and my then 33-year-old uncle called my father a traitor to the Motherland.

On the way to Panama I had my one and only case of being hit on while being suspended 30,000 feet up in the air. That was flattering mainly because no one had ever hit on me on a plane, but also because the guy offered me his phone number and told me to call him if things didn't work out with Keith. I politely declined. Obviously because I was going to visit my boyfriend for whom I had feelings but also because that was before *Up in the Air* and George Clooney making airport- and airplane-based romances sexy.

The Panamanian passport control didn't know what to make of me and my white travel document issued by the US Immigration and Naturalization Service and kept me in a tiny room for hours asking me over and over again what my citizenship was and shaking their heads over and over again when I told them I was stateless. Which was a testament to the Politburo's ingenious handbook on how to make émigrés' lives a living hell, but also a testament to Keith's patience because he was there waiting for me with flowers several hours after I landed. We spent the rest of our Panama adventure staying in windowless dives we could afford at $2 per night or crashing in the guestrooms of US Embassy diplomats who were naive enough to open their luxurious apartments with laundry facilities, views over the Pacific, and fully stocked pantries to Peace Corps volunteers who hadn't seen Twinkies or mayonnaise in months. At the end of my stay I considered "accidentally" spraying perfume into Keith's eyes again, but my bottle was empty and also, for some reason, he was staying very far away from me whenever I used it.

On his return from the Peace Corps we moved in together into a room at his mother's place, thereby causing a crisis known in my parents' house as "How dare you live with a man before marriage, are you out to shame us completely, I mean first no medical school and now this?" and known in the room we shared as "I'm not picking up the phone because I'm tired of their nagging but also what the hell are we going to do when we travel to Ohio to spend New Year's with them?" Spending New Year's with my parents wasn't negotiable, mostly because Americans didn't know how to properly celebrate New Year's but also because I wasn't heartless. Celebrating as a family has always been our tradition and, now that our family was spread across three states with my grandfather in California and my parents alone in the middle of Ohio, where the Kmart at the crossing of two interstates was the only exciting outing, it felt wrong to leave them alone.

Because by that point I had trained Keith to fully appreciate the Russian intricacies of New Year's Eve—namely "gifts are an absolute *must* on that night and who cares about Christmas or Hanukkah (although feel free to give them during those other holidays *also*, I'm not picky)"—he packed the trunk of the car we took with a large box. I internally rejoiced because I just *knew* it was a pair of Victoria's Secret pajamas I had my eye on and had pointed out to him on several occasions in the catalogue. Incidentally, pajamas were the *only* item we were able to afford from that catalogue and at $19.99, or whatever small fortune they cost in the early 90s, they were a gift reserved solely for an important occasion such as New Year's Eve. My parents put Keith up on the couch downstairs in a tiny room adjacent to the garage, clearly indicating they were not going to take part in any of the indecency that had been going on since Keith and

I met, and on the evening of the 31st we all gathered together to eat traditional Russian *zakuski*[9] and to open gifts.

Honestly, I was nervous. Opening a box with sexy pajamas in front of my parents wasn't exactly my idea of a traditional New Year's Eve and I could be reasonably sure it wasn't theirs. Still, I pressed ahead, carefully peeling off the tape to preserve that wrapping paper for the next occasion and peeking in to make sure Keith hadn't splurged and added a lingerie item into his gift. But the box contained another box and then that box contained another and then another and, by the time I had opened 204 boxes, I was exhausted and also perplexed because there was no way even the sluttiest pajamas would fit into the tiny box I unearthed after all the unwrapping.

Right. You've probably guessed where this is going, but I'm sorry to report that *I didn't.* Maybe because romantic comedies still weren't a thing on the basic cable we could afford, or maybe because I was really expecting those pajamas and was disappointed to realize Keith had paid no attention to the catalogues that showed up in our house every fortnight in which I circled the same pair *every single time*, or maybe because I was still very Soviet and had no idea that receiving a tiny box from your boyfriend was way better than any Victoria's Secret pajamas.

---

9 The Russian version of appetizers that are basically a meal in themselves because the usual set consists of about 85 salads, all smothered in mayonnaise, a collection of cold cuts and cheeses, and an aspic dish I never understood the attraction of because it's just meat and boiled carrots and sometimes a boiled egg encased in chicken gelatin (gross!).

Here are the thoughts that went through my head as soon as I unwrapped and opened that tiny box:

OMG, is this what I think it is?

Wow, it's beautiful!

Am I supposed to put it on my finger or is that his job?

When am I supposed to say yes?

Did he just ask me? Were there words coming out of his mouth just now?

I'm 23 and I'm getting married! Take that, old maidenhood in which I no longer believe of course because I'm not Soviet anymore.

Why is my mother crying? Does she still believe in it?

It doesn't matter because I don't.

Okay, the ring is on my finger and I'm going to get married.

I'm getting married to an American. *OMG I DID IT!*

And that's how my father-in-law became the proud storyteller of the "most romantic tale ever heard" (his words, not mine). He now tells the story of our meeting to everyone who asks, and then Keith chimes in with the story of how I wouldn't have gone to college had it not been for his participation at that meeting, and then his dad chimes in again to point out that Keith wouldn't have been at that meeting had he not suggested his attendance. TL;DR: the two of them think they deserve full credit for our marriage, my career, and also my driving license.

(I will prove them both wrong in the next essay titled *The Husband, Part 2*, where I also offer an in-depth look into Soviet gender dynamics.)

THE HUSBAND, PART 2, OR
SOVIET GENDER DYNAMICS: NO THANKS

My parents' joy over our impending union turned into concern five minutes after we toasted our engagement or, to be more precise, as soon as they found out that in America all wedding expenses—save for the groom's tux, I believe—were supposed to be covered by the bride's parents. Their exact words, I believe, were *"Chto oni s uma soshli?"* which translates politely as "Are you sure those are the rules?" and impolitely as "That's fucking insane." And even though at that point in time I rarely agreed with my parents on anything, I completely understood their sentiments.

Here's why:

1) We would have only been in the US for maybe four years before the wedding was to take place and three years before we had to pay for shit that would allow the wedding to take place.
2) My parents' salaries weren't enough to buy a new car, let alone a wedding menu.
3) The list of guests from our side of the family numbered in the single digits because we barely knew anyone in America and also because our family was tiny and I could count my cousins on one hand (which I didn't really need to do at that point because they weren't living in America and weren't coming anyway). TL;DR: we occupied ONE table at the wedding.

Whereas:

1) My future husband's family has been in America for generations with stable jobs, pension plans, and cars that weren't burning oil.
2) The list of guests from his side of the family numbered somewhere in three digits because apparently Americans take their cousin game *very seriously* and some cousins have their own cousins who have their own cousins and all of them want to come because weddings and funerals are the only occasions where families get together, *plus* weddings are much more fun because you get to dress up in colors and also dance to "Hava Nagila" and "YMCA." TL;DR: Keith's family took up TEN tables at the wedding.

Still, we managed to pull off that wedding without much bloodshed or even a small family feud. I was especially proud to have found a wedding dress for only $99 because it was discounted from maybe 15 seasons before and also because I found it on a sales rack in a store in rural Pennsylvania where apparently no one was getting married on a shoestring. My mother wore a hat, my grandfather cried because for the first time in his life he took part in a Jewish wedding with a real rabbi and a real *Kattubah*[1] and in a real synagogue, and my father

---

1 A Jewish marriage contract. Ours is written entirely in Hebrew, which means I still have no idea what it says, which occasionally leads my husband to claim it says things that I'm sure aren't even there like, for example, that I'm supposed to agree with him on how to correctly load the dishwasher.

blushed when we stepped out for our daughter-father dance, probably because he'd never danced in a tux or, possibly, at all.

A honeymoon was not in our budget so instead we jetted off to Uzbekistan for internships that weren't paid but were supposed to give us enough clout to find jobs that did pay after graduation. Which, as you probably know, is the whole point of the internship industry because selling hope is always better for employers than paying real money to people who are working for them. Since by then we were both in grad schools with uber exclusive names, uber expensive tuitions, and uber obscure degrees, we desperately needed that hope and were eager to pay for the privilege by adding to our student loans in an effort to finance our trip. What's another thousand or two when your north star is that future employment at a whopping $36,000 a year *in NYC*?

That was the salary I got after I graduated with the degree my parents still didn't understand. But because it was from an Ivy League university they were willing to mention it to their friends, as long as they didn't have to explain what exactly I had studied. Or what I was about to do in New York in an entry level position called a program officer, which to them sounded faintly military-like because why would anyone use the word "officer" for a desk job in a civilian non-profit organization that claimed to work on behalf of women's health? Still, they were proud I found a job so quickly after graduating, which was a lot more than could have been said for my husband. And that's how I came to look back at the year after our graduation as the year my parents' concern over our union turned into disapproval. My parents looked at that year as the year they called, "You are moving WHERE?!?!?"

Let me first paint it for you from my point of view. This is what my day was like once I started my job:

Get up at 6 a.m., wonder what possessed me to take that job, remember the student loans, the rent, the food, and an occasional pair of shoes from Marshalls (because I needed some happy moments in my life, that's why).

Get out of the house at 7 a.m., post shower, post meandering around because no human activity should take place *that* early, post grabbing a bagel or a piece of toast or even an Eggo waffle that would lose all of its crispiness while sweating in aluminum foil during my 40-minute Metro North ride to NYC.

Eat that during a brisk 30-minute walk to the office from Grand Central station.

On arrival at the office, take a seat behind a desk and work on planning programs, courses, and trips I would never run or take because even though I was an *OFFICER* I was still too young and too green (and also maybe too cocky) to *officiate* anything (*note to editor:* check if words officer and officiate are connected, otherwise rewrite this sentence).

At 5.30 p.m., the reverse trip home sans the bagel and also sans any desire to have any human conversation with anyone and especially with my parents.

At 7 p.m., arrive home and prepare to eat the dinner Keith made while spending his entire day at home looking for work.

At 8 p.m., get a phone call from my parents during which they:

- ask if Keith has a job yet
- question how long he's going to be unemployed

- demand to know why he doesn't just go get a job, ANY JOB, "I mean I worked in the construction trenches when I first got to this country and I was an engineer with years of experience stapling pipelines in Siberia, who does he think he is, there are plenty of jobs in supermarkets"
- express outrage and disgust-fueled surprise at how he, a born-and-bred-*American*, with an *American* education, *American* parents, and an *American* pedigree can't find work
- lament that their daughter has to get up at 6 a.m. and work all day while her husband—A MAN!—sits in the house doing nothing when he should be the one bringing home the bacon and she should be pregnant by now.

And during which I:

- explain for the billionth time that finding work takes time and assure them he's looking
- want to die because my parents won't ever say any of this directly to my husband's face and being in the middle sucks way worse than waking up at 6 a.m.
- remind them that long-distance calls cost money and wonder where I can move to make those calls even more expensive.

At 9 p.m. drown my misery in *Seinfeld* or *Friends* and fall asleep in the middle of an episode because 9 p.m. is nightlife and I don't do nightlife anymore.

Rinse and repeat during September, October, November, December, January, February, March, and April.

In May get a job in Uzbekistan and move there.

Now from their point of view:

September, October, November, December, January, February, March, and April: "*Kto on takoi i kakoe on imyeet pravo tak sebya vesti?*" and "*Eto vse Amerikanetzi tak'ie?*" Loosely translated: "Who the hell does he think he is?" and "Is that what you get when you marry an American?"

May: "You are moving WHERE?"

One of the major goals I set for myself long before we landed in the US was this: marry a locally born American. (And also, under no circumstances, not even if he's cute, smart, and owns several Levi's, date or fall for a man born in the Soviet Union. Meet as few of them as possible. Preferably none.[2]) I set this goal because I didn't want to marry my father. Not because I hated him, or he was a bad father, but because:

- I don't enjoy washing dishes.
- I enjoy speaking my mind and being heard.

Which was basically the antithesis of everything my father—and the larger Soviet male population—represented, thus ruling out every young man born and bred in the USSR as a potential long-term partner. To explain, here's a quick historical overview of Soviet gender dynamics.

---

2 It's a good thing we didn't end up in LA, and in retrospect I should have probably thanked my uncle for reneging on us.

SOVIET GENDER DYNAMICS: AN ILLUSTRATION

Picture a typical Soviet poster of the 1930s. On it, a woman in a red dress and red kerchief, with a smile that says she's got a list of names destined for the gulag and *you are on it*, opens a door to a brighter tomorrow. In that brighter tomorrow—drawn on a white background (subtle!)—you can glimpse modern buildings with names like "Cafeteria" and "Nursery" and "Club" and "Factory." In the foreground—also known as the "dark today" because of the black background and also because in 1931 we were all marching into the better future of communism—a woman in a blue dress is busy washing clothes while a pile of dirty dishes sits next to her. "Down with domestic slavery, bring on a new home life" the text says in large capital letters.

SOVIET GENDER DYNAMICS: AN ABSTRACT

That so didn't happen.

SOVIET GENDER DYNAMICS: AN ANALYSIS

Gender equality may have been a Soviet thing in as far as the first woman in space and women in orange vests laying railroad tracks were concerned, but gender equality was never a Soviet thing at home. Men usually came home from work, put their feet up on their sofas, picked up that day's issue of *Pravda* and read it until their wives finished making them dinner. They continued reading—or perhaps took in a Soviet news broadcast or a well-deserved nap—while their wives cleaned. The most domestically able man I knew was my grandfather, and his kitchen exploits were limited to peeling potatoes and occasionally making a tea brew. My father's claim to fame was a rare Saturday jaunt to a store from which he usually came back carrying a single loaf of bread and maybe some ground meat *if* there was no line. My friends' fathers were exactly the same.

Meanwhile our mothers did everything else. Mine cooked, cleaned, queued for toilet paper during her lunch break at work, and tended to my homework. She walked me to and from first kindergarten and then school until I turned ten and graduated to having my own key that I hung around my neck like a big girl. Taking care of homes and children was so not in the orbit of a normal Soviet male that one day my father literally forgot *to pick me up from kindergarten.* This was despite the fact that my mother reminded him that same morning that she couldn't get me, because she had to participate in the voluntary but also compulsory Party meeting loosely titled "How to increase Five Year Plan production outputs and overtake evil capitalists, and also a new edition of *BurdaModen*[3] was just smuggled in—sign-up sheet to borrow is here." When she got home that evening, she found him reading a paper in a quiet apartment *without* me in it. Then I got home five minutes later, accompanied by my kindergarten teacher who was outraged at the injustice of having to walk me home after waiting an extra hour for someone to come and get me and who, from then on, resolved to make my life a living hell because

---

3 A West German monthly complete with sewing patterns and unattainable fashion aspirations. Also known as a Soviet woman's orgasm.

Soviet kindergarten teachers weren't very nice. And also because taking their frustrations out on children was part of their professional training and, anyway, what else would a smelly kindergarten bathroom be good for if not for grounding children for the failures of their parents?

I came to several conclusions after that incident:

- Kindergarten sucked and not only because of the cold, jellified oatmeal they force-fed us in the mornings.[4]
- A box of chocolates and a deeply felt apology weren't enough to appease an angry kindergarten teacher; next time my parents should give her two boxes.
- Extracurricular Party meetings should never be scheduled in the evening. I needed to write a letter to Brezhnev about that.
- While writing that letter I should ask him to make kindergarten teachers nicer, the oatmeal warmer, and the bathrooms less smelly.

If all of the above sounds outrageous and not at all in line with the way the Soviet Union marketed its gender equality abroad, fear not! Soviet women got lots of perks for doing all this work on top of their regular jobs. Because they were members of the *slabii pol*—"the weaker sex"—they were able to enjoy:

---

4 I *still* cannot stand oatmeal. My husband thinks enough time has passed and I should let it go, but what does he know? He's never been to a Soviet kindergarten.

- boys carrying their backpacks to and from school
- men helping them with heavy bags (unless those men were strangers in which case they didn't, because honestly there weren't enough men around to assist with the heavy bags women had to carry from all the lines they stood in during their lunch breaks)
- men opening doors for them
- men letting them have their seats on public transport.[5]

In exchange, all they had to do was to be good girls and:

- work as hard as their male colleagues
- work a second shift at home—those dinners don't make themselves
- take care of children
- recognize men as the heads of families and remember to stroke their egos
- deal with their fathers making most of their decisions while unmarried
- deal with their husbands outweighing their opinions and decisions when married
- deal with mothers-in-law sticking to this status quo because if they had suffered, who are their sons' wives not to?

---

5 That was mostly the stuff of legends and old movies, which many women chose to believe but which almost always resulted in disappointment because it *never* happened.

SOVIET GENDER DYNAMICS: A CONCLUSION

There was no way I was going to tolerate any of the above outside the Soviet Union (I barely tolerated it while still there). Which is why marrying a locally born American was one of my most important goals on moving to the US—and the decision I defended, first by arguing with my parents every night on the phone, and then by going abroad to a country where calling long-distance was out of their price range.

Our move abroad marked the moment my parents' disapproval of our union turned into outright condemnation. "What kind of an American cannot get a job in America—his own damn country—who the hell did you even marry?" was one question I got from them (translation adjusted to sound more palatable). The other was: "Uzbekistan? Really?" And to be honest, the second question was understandable. Mainly because the country we were moving to was a former Soviet state and "why would you return to a place from which we just emigrated BECAUSE YOU CONVINCED US TO?" but also because they had a history with Uzbekistan they didn't think I needed to repeat. My father was sent there when he was young and just out of university to complete his *respredelenie*, which in English means "assignment" and in Soviet meant "you'll-work-wherever-the-Party-sends-you." My mother was unimpressed with leaving Moscow and my grandparents, who were very helpful with a two-year-old me. And she was even less impressed with the local kindergartens that didn't require either shoes or hats in 100+ degree heat—which is why I stood out, not only because I was the whitest child in my kindergarten group, but also because I always wore a hat, shoes, *and* socks. On the plus side, this was the first time I duly impressed my parents with my foreign language abilities, because two days after I started at the local kindergarten I was able to memorize and recite a poem about Lenin in Uzbek.[6]

Clearly my parents believed we needn't have emigrated to America for me to follow in their footsteps and go to Uzbekistan. Which I was sympathetic to, but also surprised at. Mainly because I was following in their footsteps and wasn't that something they always wanted? But my mother pointed out that they wanted this *only* when it came to me becoming a doctor, and that train had left the station unless I was going to change my mind, in which case I should stay in America and they'd pay for medical school. This was a hard no from me as I still didn't want to cut anyone open, and also cutting people open while reeling from my conversation with my parents about my jobless husband was just not safe.

In Uzbekistan, we had time to work on our marriage and conceive a child, mostly because the lights went out all the time at night and also because there were no long-distance phone calls to answer. Keith found work and, coupled with my pregnancy and a good chance they'd soon become grandparents, my parents re-blessed our union by foregoing condemnation and raising their approval rating of him from way below the US national debt to just above a zero. Then they raised it even further—past the annual GDP of China—after he took and passed the Foreign Service assessment and became a US diplomat. When I pointed out to my parents that none of this

---

6 I know my mother was impressed because she still remembers the beginning of that poem 50+ years later.

would have happened had we not gone to Uzbekistan, my mother replied, "That means he started his career in Uzbekistan just like your father did and isn't that a fascinating parallel?" At which point I thought *Let's hope this is where the similarities end* because as much as I appreciate a good omen, I didn't love that one.

YOU JUST NEVER KNOW

The first time I ignored the helpful hand of the Universe beck-oning to a brighter future and stretching towards me like the hand of God on the ceiling of the Sistine Chapel was in 1995 on a New York-bound Metro North train at 7.30 a.m. I'd like to think I ignored this potentially life-changing opportunity due to its unceremonious appearance in my life at that ungodly hour in the early morning you usually associate with chirping birds and milk bottle deliveries. I didn't function like a proper human being until around 10 a.m., and then only if I had had eight hours' sleep (that was back then when I was 20-something; now I need at least 17). But if I were to be completely honest, it most likely happened because I was still a relatively new immigrant and, thus, completely unaware of the American "Every opportunity is up for grabs" motto that came second only to "Every American gets a gun if they want one" motto. I may have also failed to pay attention to it because I've never been to the Sistine Chapel, so what would I have to compare this apparition with?

We were approaching Grand Central Station when a man sitting in front of me got up and left behind an issue of *Variety*. I had no idea what that magazine was about, but I had at least several more minutes before arriving at the station and there was no way I was giving up my seat until the train came to a complete stop. Plus, I was in the habit of checking the classifieds[1] in every periodical I saw since my husband was still looking for work months after graduating and our student loans refused to pay themselves and food cost money. But also, I wasn't happy in my own job where all I did—post uber-important Ivy League degree—was color-code training schedules for my boss and conspire with another young colleague about how one day we were going to take over and finally prove we had actually studied for a reason. (We never took over. We were wimps.)

I picked up the copy of *Variety* and turned to the classifieds. Immediately, an announcement jumped out at me: a company in Hollywood (!) was looking for a Russian speaker (!!) to work on some movie-related business with Russia (!!!). Stars danced in front of my eyes, and I'm pretty sure they weren't the Kremlin kind (although both the Hollywood boardwalk and the Kremlin stars are five-pointed so really it's a toss-up at this point in my fading memory). Here are the thoughts that went through my mind as I stared at that ad:

This sounds really interesting. Can I?

I speak Russian. I probably can.

But movies? I've never even thought of working in movies.

Who am I kidding, it'd be so much fun!

WHY am I even thinking, I should send my resume immediately.

Right. My resume is so not movie-oriented.

Besides, didn't I just spend thousands of dollars studying public health and shouldn't I at least stay long enough to pay off my student loans?

---

1 If you're a millennial or a Gen Z, this is the Stone Age (also known as the 1990s) version of whatever internet job board is all the rage at the time you're reading this.

My parents wouldn't understand.
My husband wouldn't want to move to LA.
They'd never hire me.
Forget it.

I closed the classifieds, placed the magazine back on the seat, and left the train. And I've been kicking myself ever since. Because this is what I imagine would have happened had I responded to that ad:

- I would have been called for an interview.
- I would have been hired. (Because, really fluent Russian speakers with a college education regardless of the degree were slim pickings in the US at that point. And no, I'm not being cocky—have you met me? Re-read the internal monologue above if you must.)
- I would have learned from all the great writers and directors during my long and illustrious Hollywood career.
- I would have got to work in a writers' room before I turned 80.
- I would have met Steven Spielberg.
- I would have introduced my mom to Steven Spielberg.
- My parents would have forgiven me for not going to medical school.

Instead, this is what happened:

PART 1

... in which I embark on a career because I owed it to (1) my education, which I spent an enormous amount of money on and immigrants don't give up on education they spend enormous amounts of money on; and (2) my parents, because I convinced them this was *the* profession I wanted.

After I left that copy of *Variety*, I walked 30 minutes to my then-office and spent the day making sure my color-coding pleased my boss. I did that for another 274 days and then I gave my two weeks' notice and moved to Uzbekistan. There I spoke Russian with an American accent because no local official ever took me seriously if they knew I was a Moscow-born American. I drove around in a car that always broke down in the middle of nowhere when we went on business trips to remote corners of the country, and I jammed my hotel doors with chairs in those remote corners of the country because random men thought that if they hung out by my door long enough and sweetened the deal with the bottle of *samogon* they'd bought from a guy on the corner I'd cave in and discuss Clinton politics with them. I flew in airplanes where pilots checked the fuel levels by eyeballing the inside of fuel tanks with a flashlight (if they had a flashlight), I worked for a boss who screamed at me because as an older, white male he knew everything better, and I learned that cockroaches could fly and WHAT KIND OF FRESH HELL WAS THAT EVEN?

On the plus side, I met Hillary Clinton, sat next to her, and spoke to her while I moderated a round table of women's organizations during her visit to Uzbekistan. I did that for about 30 minutes and was able, according to witnesses, to speak in complete and lucid sentences, but I retained only about a minute of that memory and it doesn't involve me speaking at all. Because in that memory, I meet her at the elevator and have trouble articulating a coherent reply to her greeting. Still, I'm proud to report that none of that stopped me from at some point writing to Bill Clinton to ask for a favor, but I'll get to that later because I'm not yet to the section where I wrap up this essay with a lesson and the moral of the story.

While in Uzbekistan, Keith found work as a local hire for the US Embassy in Tashkent, realized he'd always wanted to be a diplomat, went through the Foreign Service assessment, and passed it. This became known in our family as the start of his diplomatic career and also as one of my achievements. (My husband asked me to point out he doesn't agree with the latter, but to be fair, had we not gone to Uzbekistan, he would never have embarked on this job. Uzbekistan was where it all started—I cannot emphasize this enough. And while we're on the topic, may I just say that he never properly thanked me for that, and that some kind of appreciation would have been nice.)

PART 2

... in which I attempt to switch gears to try my luck in the career I gave up by leaving that copy of *Variety* behind WHILE also being a mother to a child and supporting a husband in his shiny diplomatic endeavors—kind of like a Hollywood-wannabe version of Julia Child but a lot less glamorous and with no aptitude for cooking whatsoever.

On our return to the US from Tashkent—with me jobless and pregnant—I spent a few months gestating my child and then giving birth to her while staying in my parents' four-bedroom plus a library plus a finished basement house and never being able to escape them or their questions as to why I couldn't get a job in America with a degree from that uber-important Ivy League university. When at some point I mentioned I was going to try writing since I'd always wanted to, my father fixed his eyes on me and asked, "How is that ever going to make you any money?" Which in retrospect was a very valid question, but I wasn't in a place where I'd allow my dream of becoming a writer to be ruined by some kind of practical consideration, so instead I decided to get offended and never mention it again. Because obviously, my parents didn't understand my poetic soul and also my brooding teenage persona had been my MO reaction to anything they said for years and, at 31, I wasn't yet ready to give it up.

During my husband's first post in Argentina I spent my toddler-free hours typing zealously into my computer what I was sure was going to become the next great American novel set in Russia. Then someone heard my great-grandmother's story that I planned to include and suggested that instead I write a screenplay.

Here's her story for background, *the long version*: In 1916, my great-grandmother's family was emigrating from Russia to Argentina when she got lost at a train station and missed her train. She was 16. For a myriad of reasons, which wouldn't fit into this book but can be summarized as "the Russian Revolution happened and everything turned into gulags," she wasn't able to join them and stayed in Russia. She got married, had my grandmother, and finally reconnected with her family in the 1960s when letters from abroad didn't always mean an immediate arrest. Then things got scary again and they lost touch. My *babushka* tried to find them in the 1980s but she never succeeded before she died.

The short version: I was named after that great-grandmother and, therefore, it was up to me to correct her mistake and to finally get our family out of Russia, which I did in 1989.

An even shorter version: We were 73 years late in getting the hell out because of one missed train connection.

A super short version: You just never know.

Because the person who heard my great-grandmother's story told me a screenplay would make for a much easier writing journey than a novel,[2] I switched gears, ordered a few books on screenwriting from Amazon (remember when Amazon *only* sold books? No? Then you're too young to be reading this book), and wrote that screenplay. When I finished it, I sent a letter to Bill Clinton because he knew Steven Spielberg, and since I'd written a screenplay I believed would be perfect for him I thought it'd be a lost opportunity if I didn't ask Bill to advocate with a mega Hollywood director on my behalf, on the basis of having met Hillary for exactly 30 minutes. (Notice my learning curve there—a long way from that nincompoop who left that copy of *Variety* on the train, right?)

That letter became my first "you just never know" moment, also known as the moment Bill Clinton's staffers got my letter, had a good laugh, did not show it to him or reach out to Spielberg on my behalf, and replied to me with a form letter. But I wasn't going to allow one disappointment to dampen my strong commitment to pipedreams. If that *Variety* fiasco taught me anything, it was that I had to take every opportunity out there, and in an effort to cement this new life motto, I contacted every Hollywood producer who'd

---

2 So not true, btw, all of you aspiring screenwriters!

ever gone to Yale. This was the era of God- and Internet-granted access to important people through your alumni website during which you could send them emails and they would *actually* reply.

While I waited for replies from those few who agreed to read my script, scrupulously bound with Acco#5 solid brass brads that the screenwriting websites told you to buy to make it in Hollywood, I went shopping. I wasn't delusional that Vera Wang would want to dress me for the Oscars and it's always good to be prepared, so I bought an outfit for the red carpet and practiced answering "Who are you wearing?" in front of the mirror. But it turned out you needed *more* than just 120 industry-standard US-letter-sized pages typed with the industry-standard 12pt courier font and bound with the industry-standard brads to make it in Hollywood, so cool your itchy fingers and don't go rushing to find me in the best dressed red carpet columns just yet. The good news, though, is that I've thrown out the brads, unbound that script, and have been editing it like my very first red carpet appearance depends on it. (Also, I still have the outfit—Hollywood, call me!)

Stubborn is my middle name[3] and so when my Oscar speech was delayed I went back to writing that novel and finished it while my husband was in between assignments and studying Russian to

---

3 My middle name is actually Vladimir, which is my dad's name and which I put as my middle name only because I was an immigrant who just stepped off the plane and how was I supposed to know that middle names were NOT patronymics? Now I'm stuck with a man's name as my middle name in my passport. PLUS, in case you forgot, I share it with Putin. So technically MY MIDDLE NAME IS PUTIN'S FIRST NAME. *Note to editor*: I just realized this should be the title of this book instead.

go to Russia, a country no one in his office ever wanted to serve in. We were the only ones to apply because he felt it would be good for his career and I thought it would be fun to go back—as an American—16 years after I left. Honestly, I don't know what possessed me but let me tell you with 100 percent certainty that being followed by Federal Security Service agents-in-training while driving through the dark streets of St. Petersburg wasn't fun. Neither was being locked out of our parking lot by an oligarch-wannabe who disapproved of how we watered our window flowers and was prepared to create an international incident because our bougainvillea were too dystrophic for his liking.

We spent our four years in Russia answering phone calls with loud breathing, checking our kitchen sink for cigarette buds the FSB usually left to let you know they were there, and resisting pulling on wires that didn't seem to belong. I spent those four years living a déjà vu in which I had no idea how to live. Sure, I spoke fluent Russian and could get into the Hermitage for one-tenth the cost other foreigners were paying, but why was this dude driving his BMW down a sidewalk with no one ticketing him? And did this woman behind the counter just say that in order to buy a cake I first have to take this tiny piece of paper on which she'd scribbled something to the cashier on the opposite side of this gigantic bakery, then stand in line to pay and receive another small piece of paper which I then have to bring back to the first woman in order to get my cake (10,000 steps right there!)? And what was up with those luxury cars with blue lights affixed to their roofs speeding against traffic on the opposite side of the road? Do they all work for Putin? Are they Putin?

As I wrestled with these questions and plotted how I'd include them in my next novel, I was also realizing I wasn't making any money from either the novel or the screenplay sitting on my computer, therefore proving my parents right. Since that wasn't something I was prepared to do, I went out and got trained as a life coach with a specialization in expats, or as I defined the niche, people with expendable income. My training and certification was through a coaching school dubbed the "Harvard" of coaching and so, for the price of a small luxury car, I got my second Ivy League degree and was able to call myself a life coach, a.k.a. a person who wasn't a therapist, but who felt strongly that coaches were an evolved species of therapists because [insert the spiel that the "Harvard" coaching school provided us with, which I no longer remember].

With another uber-distinguished education under my belt, making lots of money was the next logical step if I were to impress my parents and convince them that their immigrant dream for me was still not dead. And so for the next several years I did everything that coaches who coached coaches (a requirement if you ever want to get certified—any red flags there yet?) recommended, namely: put up a website to attract clients, gave talks to attract clients, wrote newsletters to attract clients, gave freebies to attract people to sign up for those newsletters, created while-you-sleep content in several languages, opened an online academy for cross-cultural training, sold courses on "how to work and live" in 18 countries created by consultants I'd hired, designed a teaching algorithm to help clients work effectively across borders, and exhausted myself for less than $1000 per month, in a *good* month.

That seemed like a really low minimum wage for running a business I wasn't enjoying—if you could even call it a business since it was more like a hobby because I did it practically for free and shouldn't hobbies be enjoyable and a lot less stressful and time consuming? So I put together a survey and sent it to coaches working in my field of clients with expendable income to see how many of us were making a living wage. Sure, this wasn't a huge sample but hey, if your results come back and you see that less than 10 percent of your colleagues are pulling in a salary on which you could probably live in a rural Ohio town circa 1960, and the rest are making enough for a nice dinner out, you start questioning things. You continue to question things when the only people answering in the affirmative about making a decent living in that "Harvard" coaching Facebook group are COACHES WHO ARE COACHING COACHES. Did someone say Ponzi scheme?

PART 3

... in which my career takes the turn it was supposed to take on that Metro North train.

I retired from coaching with a bang by writing a scathing personal essay about why I quit coaching, and that was my very first freelance writing assignment for which I got paid. I wrote more essays after that—none of them about coaching, mainly because I was done with that but also because Twitter hate is real—and I tinkered with a novel I began plotting in my free-from-coaching time back when I was living the Russian déjà vu. The novel explored the important themes of identity, of what happens when you come back to a country you left more than a decade ago, of how you reconcile who you were then with who you are now… Wait, what? SORRY, NO! I got confused there for a moment. That was the novel I probably should've written but didn't, since I spent an inordinate amount of time wondering if the guy living above us was a real oligarch or just a mini one, agonizing about whether the FSB was going to poison my dog Pushkin because they definitely could, and figuring out how to buy cakes without short-circuiting my Fitbit.

So instead of a deep, philosophical, Booker Prize-worthy epic, I wrote a fun, satirical novel about Putin and his henchmen. Because I was smart and didn't want to find nerve agents in my tea, I wrote it under a pen name. By that point I was living in Madrid so I work-shopped that novel with the best writing group I've ever had (hey, Madrid Writers Club circa 2012–14) and, unlike my previous novel, which is still occupying 137KB of space on my hard drive, this one got published. I had a book launch, served some Russian candy during it for authenticity, and then sat back and waited for the royal-ties to roll in, movie contracts to fall into my lap, *Variety* people to get in touch, and my bank account to expand to the respectable enough number of zeros to show my parents. I also took my Oscar outfit to the dry cleaners—you can never be too prepared for the red carpet.

NONE OF THAT HAPPENED, THOUGH.

But you already knew this, right? (I mean, apparently my dad knew, so you must have!) None of it happened because (1) I'm not J.K. Rowling; (2) Putin got hold of the manuscript and sent his people around to make sure no one bought the book (I'm sure of it!); and (3) the publishing house that published it was a tiny outfit whose idea of marketing was to list the book on Amazon and see what happened. Their idea of management and everything else that had to do with the publishing business was just as professional and that's why two years after my novel came out most of their authors, including me, took their rights back. My book now lives on as an "out of print" title (offers to re-print it are welcome!) but the good news is that I'm no longer hunted by Putin and his people.

While all of this was happening, I was practicing my "you just never know" motto by sending my essays everywhere in the known world. Those were the years of the personal essay, and editors at large, national publications were actually reading, complimenting, and publishing my work. Soon I graduated to features and reported pieces, which was so much more than I ever expected from myself, but definitely not as much as my parents expected of me—partially because they still hadn't met Spielberg, but mainly because they continued to think I did nothing all day, every day. My mom told me this once in a conversation where I suggested they sell their beachfront condo in Miami because they don't know how to drive a gondola and Miami will soon be Venice. "You should get a real estate license," she said. "Then you can sell it and earn a commission. *Vse ravno delat' nechego.*" Which is Russian for, "You've got nothing to do anyway" and my parents for, "We still have no idea what you've done with your life so, here, have a real estate commission and put something on your resume that will qualify at least as remotely successful and also earn you some money."

I wanted to point out that being published in large national publications without any writing education and while writing in your second language was probably more of a qualification for success than selling a condo in Florida, but my parents aren't very familiar with the US media landscape because they now have access to

Russian television and why would anyone need any more news? Besides, freelance writing is confusing if your only reference for a freelance is that Soviet illegal furniture maker whose phone number you guarded like a state secret both because of the demand for well-made kitchen furniture and also because if the authorities got wind of what he was doing he'd be logging wood in Siberia instead of making kitchen sets out of that wood. All of this is to say that it took me a whole hour-and-a-half to explain to my mother what it meant to be a freelance writer, but I don't think I succeeded since in the end she asked if I get a "writerly" salary like in the Soviet Union, where all respected writers were members of the Union of Writers which paid them salary, but also voted them out of the Union if they wrote anything remotely anti-Soviet.

To conclude, if you ask me what I'm most afraid of, I'd probably say bogeymen hiding in my closet, snakes, and lost opportunities. The last one is hard to define with precision (unlike snakes which are very, very clear, as are bogeymen) but it basically means that, since the *Variety* debacle, I believe in taking advantage of *all* the opportunities that come my way and trying everything. For example, the other day I spent an hour convincing my daughter to apply for an internship she didn't think she could get, insisting there was at least a 0.0000000001 percent chance she would get it. Hope always defies logic, and back in the old country if we didn't have hope, we didn't have anything. In Russian, there is a saying, *Nadezhda umiraet poslednei*—Russian for "Hope is the last to die" and former Soviet for "Don't waste an opportunity" and "Keep dreaming" joined together. Which is basically the same thing as "You just never know."

TAK VOSPITALA, OR KARMA IS A BITCH

Every time my college-age daughter fails to call me for longer than a week, I think my mother secretly rejoices. Partially because she can now cite this as the proper punishment for my own youthful failure to speak to her every day (really, saying karma is a bitch is a lot faster, but my mother *never* swears) but mainly because she can now say, "I told you so." Actually, it sounds more like "*Tak vospitala,*" which is Russian for "It's your own fault because you've failed in your parenting because you decided not to listen to me and instead chose to parent your own way."

I'm an overachiever so it'll come as no surprise that I started failing at parenting even before my daughter was born. That was because I didn't do the right thing when choosing her name and, by the right thing, I mean consider my parents' opinion about her name and, by consider their opinion, I mean give her the name they thought was right.

A little bit of a background: in the Soviet Union when you had a baby there were many important issues to solve and questions to answer.

1) How much of a bribe to give to procure a pram, a crib, and a pacifier?
2) Do we give it to the same guy or do we spread the goodness?

3) How much tea with milk should I drink for my milk to come in?

4) Which maternity house can I get into with *blat* or which one is closer without?

5) Is this rope thick and stable enough to pull things up to the seventh floor of the maternity house? Can it safely bring up liquid, because my mother-in-law makes a mean *borsht*? What if my husband is tasked with tying the pot to the rope? Because God only knows, *otkuda u nego ruki rastut*, he's a mechanical engineer but cannot fix a chair to save his Party membership.

6) How do I walk to the window to show my family our new addition if everything hurts? Will the nurse do it for me for a rouble? Will she do it for five roubles for the next seven days I'm imprisoned in this dump of a building where no one is allowed to visit because babies can catch a cold but where cockroaches crawl around like they own the place (they do) because they were here first?

7) Why are these mashed potatoes green?

8) Whose baby is this and why is s/he at my breast?

If you were a Jewish woman having a Jewish baby anytime between 1952 and 1989, you had an additional issue to solve:

9) What do we call this offspring of ours if we want to pay homage to the Jewish tradition of naming a child after a deceased relative, but don't want to pay homage to the Russian

tradition of being an antisemite's punching bag because the name is *way too* Jewish-sounding?

Contrary to what my literary friends think, I wasn't named after Bulgakov's *The Master and Margarita* (although that would have made for a much sexier story because the novel is a literary masterpiece and also who wouldn't want to be named after a witch who flew naked through Stalinist Moscow while inflicting revenge on party *aparatchiks* who may have sent your uncle to a gulag?). Instead, I was named after my great-grandmother Rivka but, because her name was so Jewish it could raise a dead Cossack out of his grave on the promise of a satisfying pogrom alone, my family only used the first letter of her name. That's how I became Rita, short for Margarita. And, really, their ingenuity deserves a lot of credit: I had a whole nine years of complete bliss of no one calling me *zhidovka*! (Also worth mentioning here is that after moving to the US, I spent 30+ years of my life collecting a quarter for every pizza and drink joke made at my expense and that's why I now own a small island. Yay, Soviet antisemitism and its unintended consequences?)

I found out the sex of my child as soon as I technologically could (don't get me wrong, I like surprises but just not when you're sprawled out on a delivery table with your privates exposed) and immediately my parents demanded she'd be named after my *babushka* Betya. I promptly rejected that idea, because as much as I wanted to name my daughter after my *babushka*, this was the twenty-first century and wouldn't it amount to child abuse to give her a name that made the most popular girl names list when the last Russian Tsar was still alive? But because I loved my grandmother and because guilt was an emotion that drove most of my decisions pre-menopause, my husband and I drove to Barnes & Noble (remember when those were *within* driving distance?) where we sat on the floor for three hours leafing through every baby book they carried and looking for names that started with a B.

We didn't find *any* we liked. There must have been hundreds but obviously none were good enough for that tiny cherub who was years away from slamming doors but was already excelling at causing family rifts.

When we did find a name we both loved, it wasn't in the B category. It started with an E and when I pointed that out my husband said, "But that's even better because we can name her both after my grandmother, whose name was Esther, and after yours because E is almost the same as B." I wondered if this was a sign of early glaucoma or if he really didn't know the English alphabet as well as I did. I also realized he could never say this aloud because my parents would disown me for choosing his grandmother over mine. So we made up a middle name that started with a B (because really there were *no* good names in those books even for a middle name!) and then put Eliana and B***[1] together in a Soviet kind of formation where last name always preceded the first name. That was key because my *babushka*'s maiden name started with E and her first name started with a B. I pointed out this similarity to my parents, claiming that

---

1 My daughter requested that I didn't disclose her middle name because she thinks it's the ugliest name she's ever heard. I take issue with that sentiment, mostly because I was the one to make it up but also because I still think it's pretty.

even though my daughter's first name wouldn't begin with a B, this whole arrangement was like *pyatiletka v chetyre goda²* because our daughter would have *two* names honoring *babushka*. Which was obviously better than one and I thought that logic was impenetrable. But they didn't buy it at all (possibly because the metaphor was outdated, but most likely because this was completely against everything they believed in) and for the first five years they called my daughter by her middle name.

The grave mistake I made in naming this child cemented my parents' fear that I was doomed as a parent. My mother sprung to help, thus beginning a period in my life that I named, "Don't pick up the phone." She called every day, wherever in the world we happened to be, and inquired about the following:

1) What Eliana had for breakfast.
2) What she had for lunch.
3) What she had for dinner.
4) How much fish she had ("I cannot believe you are forcing my grandchild to adopt your ridiculous vegetarian diet and depriving her of meat, how can you call yourself a responsible mother, did you at least make sure she has fish with every meal?").
5) How many fruits and vegetables she consumed.
6) How many fruits and vegetables I consumed without sharing with her.
7) How many walks she had and for how long.

---

2 Russian for completing a five-year plan in four years and Communist for overachieving (but Soviet reality for "this chair has uneven legs").

8) How many walks I had without taking her.

9) How many after-school activities she was signed up for and whether I had enrolled her into ballet and piano.

10) Why the rest of her first-grade class all had iPhones and she didn't, and what kind of mother was I to deny my daughter what everyone else had?

11) Ditto for Kindle and iPad.

12) Ditto for the priciest Abercrombie & Fitch outfits.

13) Ditto for a brother, or a sister, or both.

With time, questions 1 through 8 migrated to conversations my mother held directly with my daughter, and I breathed a sigh of relief because I could stop keeping a diary of what I fed my child and maybe occasionally order a pizza. Questions 10 through 12 lost their relevance when my parents classified me as a cheapskate and began buying my daughter everything she asked for. This is approximately how that worked:

ELIANA: Can I have the iPhone [the-latest-shiny-model] for my birthday or New Year's, please?

PARENTS: If your mom agrees and also if you have all A grades and maybe just one B.

ME: I don't even have the iPhone [the-latest-shiny-model] yet!

PARENTS: It'll be an incentive for her, why not?

ME: FINE.

ELIANA [brings home one A, three Bs, and a C.]

PARENTS: Here's your iPhone, sweetie.

Question 13 stopped after I had three miscarriages in three years and then—just so that the Universe could teach me a lesson, because really how many signs from heaven do you need that you shouldn't try for any more offspring—I got diagnosed with breast cancer. To drive the point home, and because more is always better in the when-it-rains-it-pours sense,[3] my mother got diagnosed with the same cancer *that same week*. We shared a hospital room, a breast surgeon, and a plastic surgeon, which, honestly, added up to more things in common than the number of opinions we'd shared at that point. My husband shaved his head in solidarity, which terrified our then six-year-old daughter more than when I shaved mine (because I look better with a shaved head), but Eliana took this whole scenario of both her mother and her grandmother going through a life-threatening disease like a champ and only occasionally threw tantrums. Which drove my father up the wall because he likes quiet and Eliana had a knack for out-screaming the Fox News (proud mama here!) he always had on in the background.[4]

---

3 I'm working on these *humorous* essays while: (1) Covid is obliterating humanity; (2) my husband is undergoing a lymphoma treatment; (3) we aren't in our home as he gets his treatment because our home is in Athens, Greece, from which we had to be med-evacuated because he has the *rarest* type of lymphoma ever, and no one knows how to treat it there; (4) it's cloudy and cold here while it's sunny and warm in Athens where I would have been now writing on a patio and listening to birds sing; (5) Trader Joe's is a 30-minute walk away, why is life so unfair?

4 I should probably mention here that at the time of my and my mother's diagnoses we shared their house because I was diagnosed with breast cancer while in Russia on my husband's assignment, and there was no way I was going to entrust cancer to the Russian health care system, private or not. We moved in with my parents into their

Since doctors always did a double-take when my mother and I showed up for our appointments together, they tested me for one of those BRCA genes that causes breast cancer. And since the Universe doesn't joke around when it unloads misery, I was positive for it. I blame my ancestors—couldn't they mix it up a little? I mean, I get it if you have an attractive first cousin and you live one street away from each other and no one grows a beard like that cousin does, but come on? The worst of it, of course, was thinking my daughter might also have inherited that gene and even though she had that elusive 50 percent chance of not getting it from my husband, by that point I was pretty sure the Universe had it in for me and would have given it to her just because it could.

After several chemo treatments that made me want to throw up all of my insides and never eat again, I came to the conclusion that whatever I could cut out to *never* go through any of this again, I'd rip out of my body, no regrets, no questions asked, no anesthesia needed. I removed both breasts *and* both ovaries and would have removed more had the doctors not stopped me because, really, I just needed the bare minimum to remain on this Earth long enough to see my daughter get a new iPhone every year into eternity, or at least until Apple came up with something even better.

---

four-bedroom, three-bathroom, one library, a finished basement, a sitting room, a living room, a dining room, and a large deck house, but that cohabitation didn't last long because it was *too small a space for two families*. And my father is against small spaces as much as he's against noise and the smell of cooked garlic. Which, honestly, is crazy because that's one of the most delicious smells in the world.

Then the teen years hit and I wondered if I had made the right decision because if hell was real and if I ended up there on exiting Earth, it could not have been any worse than what I was living when my daughter turned 12-and-a-half (she's an overachiever, like me). Our apartment must have felt these vibes because the walls did *not* enjoy crumbling when she slammed the doors. Likewise, the doormen didn't enjoy the yelling coming out of our house. And I did not appreciate it when she used ketchup to smear on her pads to avoid going to swimming lessons and I *actually* believed she had her period. (In my defense, I don't eat enough ketchup to recognize it when applied to a pad by an ingenious teenager and also, by that point in my life, I hadn't had a period for a few years so how was I even supposed to remember that menstrual blood doesn't look like ketchup?)

But the worst part of her adolescent outbursts wasn't the bruised ego of a grown-ass woman who was period-bamboozled by a child. It was a much deeper discontent. As I navigated this *Titanic* of our mother–teen experience, I was realizing with horror that we were heading right for the iceberg of my relationship with my parents, because I was steering that doomed liner like they did with me. If this metaphor is too literary, there's an easier way to say this: I was becoming my parents. Also known as: too critical, often judgmental, full of expectations, and a solid gold medal candidate in the "because I told you so and because this is what you need to do for me to look good in the world" parental Olympics. When one day she called me a "Russian mother" I spent the whole evening crying on the floor of my kitchen while salmon burned in the oven. Not only because she also told me to "go die in a hole" but also because being a Russian mother was exactly what I had decided *not* to be when she was born, and why was this unnecessary Russian-ness oozing out of me now, more than two decades after I'd left? Did I completely fail in assimilation? Was this Putin's fault too?[5]

Meanwhile everyone blamed me for Eliana's behavior. My parents blamed me because "Who's to blame?" was Lenin's go-to question and they were sticking to it, and also because this proved they were right about my subpar parenting. My husband blamed me because he was at work during the day and came home to a fight instead of a glass of whiskey, a cooked meal, and a foot rub, I guess? His exact words to me were "You're an adult and you should know better," which I honestly didn't appreciate because no adult can deal with a teenager on their own and it takes a supportive village and I didn't have one. We'd just moved to Madrid and the only people I knew there were our doormen and the vendors at the nearby market where I escaped during the day to buy bread and fish and vegetables and also to drink wine with lunch because it was Spain and they know how to live life.

Since our daughter was smart (plus it doesn't take a nuclear physics degree to figure out how to manipulate a parent when that parent disagrees with the other one on parenting matters *in front* of the child they are parenting), she took full advantage of the situation and played my husband like Maradona played that hand of God. And he went along with it most of the time because he wanted to be the "good cop" parent, the equation that automatically made me into the "bad cop" parent and that wasn't the designation I wanted

---

5 Not at all out of the left field because Putin *was* everywhere then and he's still everywhere now.

to have because (1) that's not an effective parenting strategy, any child psychologist would tell you this (ours did); (2) coupled with the "Russian mother" this was too much responsibility, I was *not* the KGB; and (3) how was she ever going to love me when I was the only one dispensing boundaries and rules and in general, you know, PARENTING?

We had to make some changes, but my husband was completely against relinquishing his "good cop" persona and presenting a united front. Mainly because he enjoyed being the preferred parental unit, but also because he probably thought supporting me would make him more of a Russian, which in turn would bring him closer to Putinism and further from, you know, American exceptionalism. Our child psychologist then suggested a boarding school and her exact words were, "They'll enforce the rules so that you don't have to," and she said that looking at me. At which point I wanted to hug her because that was the first time anyone had recognized how hard it was to enforce the rules *all by yourself* and also because I could finally stop crying on the floor of my kitchen and burning food in the oven, which, by then, I was doing almost every night.

For my parents, the boarding school decision drove the last nail into the coffin of me as a good mother—kind of like *perestroika* and *glasnost* finished the Soviet Union and with it, Gorbachev's career. My mother said "How could you?" and meant "Motherhood is about suffering. You should have suffered some more and raised your own child instead of unloading her onto someone else and also I breastfed you when my nipples were cracked and bleeding and you can't cry on the floor a few nights? And anyway, if you're crying you are doing something wrong." Which was a perfect demonstration of how to be critical, judgmental, and full of expectations all at the same time; and, honestly, I cannot thank my mother enough for this timely reminder. Because I used the weekends when our daughter came home to do exactly the opposite and since I no longer had to enforce any rules and watch those rules get trampled by my husband's "good cop" strategy, I dare say I succeeded. I'm not saying I became a perfect, non-Russian mother because, truth be told, Russian-ness doesn't die easy, but I'm proud of myself for curbing the worst of those tendencies. And that's really more than one can say for the 2016 US elections and the whole Trump presidency, because there was more Russian influence in it than in my entire parenting journey, and I'm not done yet.

My child has now been legal to drink in Europe for three years and in the US for a few months, and she's great. We still have our disagreements, but for the most part our *Titanic* has safely made it across the Atlantic not once, but several times. Last time it happened was when she got a nose ring and my mother stopped speaking to her because Eliana didn't respect her opinion on not getting her nose pierced and that opinion was based on "because I told you so and because this is what you need to do for me to look good in the world," the world being my parents' condo building. At which point I called my mother and explained that (1) it was Eliana's body and she could do what she wanted with it; and (2) who cares about what other people think? My mother protested by saying that she cared, and I was transported back to my childhood when other people's judgments mattered too much, which was partially what crashed our *Titanic*, if I was going to use that metaphor again. This led me to ask her how important her relationship with her granddaughter was to her, and if it was more important than her relationship with people she sometimes saw at the beach, and my mother had to admit I was right. Which I took as a sign that I actually won at parenting and that my mother no longer thought I sucked as a mother.

PS: Eliana, if you're reading this, please call your *babushka*. She hasn't heard from you in more than a week.

THE SHOULD-HAVE-DONE-IT BUCKET LIST

I'm the oldest person in my graduate program at the University of Oxford. I'm pretty certain of this, even though the one and only time I saw my classmates was through those tiny Microsoft Teams windows on a 13-inch laptop screen. But I spent just as much time comparing everyone else's jowls to mine as I spent listening to our workshop leaders (*note to my editor:* take this fact out please, I do want to get my degree) and mine are definitely a lot more southbound. I won't go into neck issues, because then I'd be channeling Nora Ephron and she doesn't need channeling. She's Nora Ephron, for Pete's sake.

To be clear, I don't feel bad about my jowls. They are there for a reason and having southbound jowls means I'm still around and that's good news. Another piece of good news is that I *am* an Oxford student and, lest there was some intergalactic meddling during which aliens from a faraway planet intervened on my behalf, I've been accepted into the university rated best in the world for five years running because apparently *I'm worthy.* Which, I'll have you know, is an alien thought for any writer (that's why I think aliens must have been involved). Most writers have such crippling impostor syndrome that they never fail to mention it in interviews. And because those interviews are meant for the writerly crowd, what usually follows of course is advice on how to overcome it, which I normally don't heed because I already know how to deal with mine:

1) Wake up in a bad mood because your last day's writing didn't go well.
2) Snap at your loved ones.
3) Refresh your email for the 15th time in case your editor replied to that draft you sent last night.
4) Refresh your email in case an agent replied to the query letter you sent last year.
5) Scan Facebook, Twitter, and Instagram for *any* mention of you or your writing.
6) Don't find any because apparently your writing sucks and no one likes it.
7) Rinse and repeat until your phone battery dies.
8) Open your laptop and have another go at the writing you hated from yesterday.

Being the oldest student on your course has its advantages and disadvantages. Let's start with disadvantages, because it's always good to end on a positive note. I don't know if it has been scientifically proven but an older person's brain usually shrivels to accommodate the fewer number of fucks they now give about things that seem of the utmost importance to the younger folks. Although this is normally an advantage, in my case the shriveled brain is a bit of a chore, because for the last month I haven't been able to understand WHAT THE HELL THE YOUNG'UNS HAVE BEEN JOKING ABOUT on our course's WhatsApp chat. In other words, I'm not too fast on the uptake. (They're now probably WhatsApping behind my back about how I'm ignoring them, and about my jowls. But honestly, I don't give a fuck. You see how this works?)

Now let's move to the advantages. I'm about the same age as half of my tutors and older than the other half. Which can only mean they will approach me with some appreciation for all the wisdom I've accumulated over the years. Because nothing screams "the most committed student ever" like a middle-aged woman who already has a master's degree in a field she's barely worked in and who's changed careers three times. Another advantage is that I've been around long enough to have actually witnessed the collapse of the USSR *without* wearing a diaper or playing with toy soldiers. And that I can write about this and about smuggling jewelry through Soviet customs while those were still a thing.[1]

But the biggest advantage is that studying creative writing is actually the last item I got to cross out on my should-have-done-it bucket list.[2] If you've never heard of this before, that's because I invented the term. The should-have-done-it bucket list is the list of things you regret *not* doing because someone or something (read: your family, the culture you were born into, your fear of raisins)

---

1 I won a contest with that story and you can read it *on a bag*. Yes, an actual tote bag. Then you can pile your Trader Joe's groceries into it and feel all smug because you own literary bags.

2 Unless you count taking a trip on the Trans-Siberian railway, which I should have done before but cannot now because I wrote a book making fun of Putin. And because the FSB *knows* who I am and I'm not crazy enough to walk right into their clutches just to ride a train for seven days and seven nights without a shower. I'm too old for that. Both for the FSB and the no-shower thing.

prevented you from doing them. And because I'm wise, I'm going to go ahead and recommend that you DON'T have one.

I wrote my list as soon as I turned 40 because 40 is that magical number that exponentially reduces the number of fucks you give about guilt or disapproval or the number of sighs your mother emits in a phone conversation with you. Because life is complicated and because, between the time I turned 40 and now, I moved three countries, raised a teenager, and tried not to kill her in the process, I didn't get around to crossing this last item off my list until now. But I did it anyway, even though I'm old and my brain is shriveled and words like "esoteric" and "sangfroid" send me to a dictionary in panic. All of this is to say that I really, really want to study creative writing. Which means I plan on being very committed to my studies (this is just in case my tutors didn't believe me up above) and memorizing every word that scares me now.

I wasn't always committed to writing. That was mainly for two reasons: (1) Soviet teachers and (2) Soviet parents. I'll start with the teachers, because when we were growing up we weren't allowed *ever* to question the teachers. I'm just making up for lost time.

Most Soviet teachers fell into two camps—flustered or scary. Our Russian language and literature teacher was scary. She usually walked into the classroom with her neck askew like a hawk, her large wire glasses perched on her pointy nose, and her stare steely as if she was practicing to be Stalin.[3] Most of the time she didn't teach us anything, so we copied forewords and called them essays. I'm not proud

---

3 A little bit of history (you're welcome): Stalin was born with the surname Jughashvili, which didn't make it easy to run the USSR

of this but, also, I never got caught so I guess that's something to be proud of? Not that it was easy to catch plagiarism then—Google's Sergey Brin wasn't born yet and there were plenty of forewords to go around from all the editions of Pushkin, Tolstoy, and Dostoevsky littering our neighborhood libraries.[4] Come to think of it, maybe that's why Brin invented Google. Maybe his mother or grandmother was a Russian literature teacher. (*Note to self:* look up Brin's biography. Also maybe ask him to write the blurb for this book.)

Then one day my luck ran out. No, I didn't get caught for plagiarizing. But I got caught for something equally as scandalous (apparently!):

ME [with a smirk and the attitude of a 16-year-old who knows everything]: I don't really care about Russian literature. I'm going into the technical field. I won't need it.

MY FRIEND [nodding in agreement]: Lucky you.

I got a 2^5 for my next essay. And another 2 for the essay after that. And after that. When I brought home my third disgrace, my mother decided to take matters into her own hands. She marched to our school, a box of chocolates in her bag, and asked the teacher

---

with an iron fist so he went ahead and changed it to Stalin, the word derived from *stal'*, Russian for steel.

4 I still sometimes have nightmares of not having returned one of those to the library before I emigrated and I wake up in a cold sweat after being chased by an army of Soviet librarians who were just as scary as our Russian literature teacher.

5 The equivalent of an F for an American and the equivalent of the end of the world for my parents.

why her daughter, who until then had been bringing 4s[6] for those plagiarized essays (to be clear, my mother didn't mention they were plagiarized), was now only getting 2s. The box of chocolates was a bribe; you didn't go anywhere in the Soviet Union without a bribe. The value of your bribe depended on your economic level, with a box of chocolates reserved for the Soviet middle class intelligenzia. (Foreign soap was also a thing, as were bottles of Armenian cognac.)

The teacher explained, eyes owl-wide and shaking her head, that she overheard me trashing Russian literature. *Sacrilegious*, she meant to communicate. (*Note to the legal team:* I'm pretty sure that teacher is no more, but if she is, please don't tell her I named my dog Pushkin.) My mother wrung her hands, added a pleading look at her box of chocolates, and negotiated a truce. That's how I found my name being called the moment the teacher walked into the classroom the next day.

TEACHER: GOKUN.

ME [standing up]: Yes?

THE ENTIRE CLASS (including the boy I had a terrible crush on) [staring with that mix of curiosity, pity, and fear—the same exact kind of stare my great-uncle got when they took him to the gulag]

TEACHER [walking to her desk, gold earrings swinging in her ears[7]]: Why did Tolstoy have Anna Karenina kill herself at the end?

---

6 A B in America and a "sigh-but-okay" in my house.

7 Rumor had it this was the bribe from my crush's parents. They were upper-class Soviet bureaucrats. Chanel N°5 was another option for their kind.

ME [praying that boy cannot see red because I'm turning the color of cooked beet all the way from my ears to my cheeks to my neck]: ...

I'm not going to recount the answer, mostly because I can't remember what I said, but also because it was some Soviet propaganda bullshit I'd gleaned from a foreword the night before. My mother had told me I'd be called on to answer a question and I spent the hours I usually spent staring at the phone willing that boy to ring me memorizing forewords. Because I had a good memory, I passed. The teacher began grading all of my essays at a 3 level, which is like a C but with a lot of parental heartbreak. My mother wondered if the box of chocolates was past its prime because those 3s were accompanied by a Baikal Lake of red-ink comments that pointed out my ineptitude in all things written. I never again said anything about Russian literature aloud. And I wrote off all possibilities of me writing ever again.

Here I should point out that it wasn't really up to me to write it off. Even if I were the Evgeny Kissin of literature,[8] even if I knew then that I wanted to become a writer, and even if that teacher hadn't killed any desire I may have had to put words on paper, I wouldn't have gone into writing. I also wouldn't have gone into performing. Or into art. Or into any kind of career that didn't involve a math entrance exam, a study of thermodynamics, or an encounter with

---

8 A Soviet musical child prodigy and my worst nightmare. Mostly because as a child of Soviet intelligenzia I was required to learn piano, but I was completely tone deaf. Disappointment doesn't even begin to describe what my parents felt when they heard me touch the keys.

cadavers at a Moscow morgue. Which is to say I had a choice that limited me to becoming either an oil and gas engineer or a doctor.

I was not *banned* from studying something else. Not technically, anyway. Conceivably, I could have told my parents that I wanted to become an actress (I did do a mean interpretation of blue-haired Malvina, Buratino's[9] girlfriend, in school) or the nation's next Isaak Babel[10] or a sculptor of Lenin busts (I was very good at sketching statues and because Lenin's was basically everywhere, I perfected that almost to the level of plagiarizing forewords). Even more conceivably, they would have looked at me and laughed. Not because they didn't believe in me, but because *engineers didn't give birth to artists in the Soviet Union*. And artists didn't give birth to engineers. I mean, there were six engineers in my family, one doctor, and zero artists of any kind. As a Soviet child, you followed in the footsteps of your parents and grandparents: those were the rules. And we didn't make the rules. If you were related to physics geniuses and math whizzes, you couldn't go on sculpting Lenin, even if you were better at that than at math.

I didn't want to be a doctor. I didn't want to be an engineer either, but designing pipelines and gas storage facilities were easier to stomach than plucking eyeballs out of cadavers. Of course, I couldn't tell my family I wasn't interested in following in my *babushka*'s foot-

---

9 A Soviet version of Pinocchio that introduced the proletariat and class struggle into the story. In case you are interested, it all ended well, with Bolsheviks in power.

10 I wouldn't be allowed to become the nation's next Tolstoy because Tolstoy was Russian and *everyone* in the Soviet Union knew a Jew could never be Russian.

steps because of my nerves. You weren't supposed to have nerves as a Soviet child. Unless they were nerves of steel, of course.

Another reason I couldn't turn down this career in medicine was my mother and her dreams, understandably invested with all the vigor of a Jewish parent into her only child. Turned out she had always regretted not becoming a doctor and now that she had a daughter, she could easily fix that regret. BY MAKING ME DO IT. Easy peasy. Just inject me with one of those anesthetics the Soviet Union never had for surgeries and let me sail through my medical training asleep.

To tell my mother I wasn't going to study medicine was to tell her I was renouncing her as a mother. Obviously I wasn't going to hurt someone who wished me so much good; I'm not an asshole. So I had to come up with a strategy that would inflict the least amount of pain while ensuring the best outcome for me. I turned to antisemitism.

In those days (as in all previous days—or at least since the Doctor's Plot in 1952[11]) Soviet medical schools had quotas for Jews. The fact that Jews make the best doctors[12] somehow escaped the Soviet government, and for a Jewish person to get into a medical school required a lot of favors, mainly in the form of black caviar, gold jewelry, and Bolshoi tickets. Grades were important too, of course,

---

11 During which my grandmother was accused of wanting to kill Stalin and sat in her office wondering if she had enough time to finish examining the one patient who dared to see her before a car came to take her to the gulag.

12 That's according to every Jewish mother *everywhere*.

but there, unfortunately, I was lacking in argument. For reasons I couldn't explain, my biology teacher always gave me 5s—the highest mark in the Soviet system—even though I knew nothing about biology. I suspect that was because her name was also Margarita and, thinking we were both named after a witch,[13] she felt a certain degree of solidarity with me.

When it came to medical school, my parents and grandparents were willing to empty their Sberbank accounts and sell their Soviet souls for *Swan Lake*:

FAMILY: We have two large cans of caviar and know people at the furniture warehouse who know people at the confectionery factory who know people at the Bolshoi.

ME: [armed with antisemitism and channeling my inner Rasputin, who, incidentally, was a rabid antisemite but was also very good at convincing people to do what he wanted them to do]: Still, those quotas. And what about the entrance exams? What if I fail them? And you would have asked so many people for favors?[14]

---

13 This reference is from *The Master and Margarita* in which Margarita (after whom I wasn't named as you've already discovered in a previous essay) strips naked and flies through 1930s Moscow wreaking havoc on Stalin's henchmen. Basically, the dream of every Soviet citizen who wasn't an asshole.

14 Asking people for favors and then not acing entrance exams was much worse than selling your Soviet souls for *Swan Lake*. Mainly because not acing exams meant failing, and failing in front of others was pure *pozor*, which means shame in English and I'd-rather-dis-own-you-than-suffer-this-kind-of-embarrassment in the language spoken by all Soviet-Jewish parents.

FAMILY [pensive]

ME [celebrating inside]

Unfortunately, my celebrations were premature. Because while my parents didn't make me go to medical school in Moscow, they insisted I go to one in the US when two years later I convinced them to emigrate (antisemitism wasn't working so well for me—or for any Soviet-Jewish person—anymore, hence the second wave of Jewish immigration in 1989, which I started).[15] Their conditions were clear. If my father was going to agree to move halfway around the world,[16] I had to promise it would be worth it. And the only promise that would stand was if I went to medical school, completed my mother's dream, and became a doctor.

For which I'm very, very sorry. Not for never becoming a doctor but for agreeing I'd do it and then changing my mind. But how else was I going to convince them to leave the cesspool of antisemitic bigotry that USSR was quickly becoming? And also, how was I to know that once I landed in the US I'd be met with such an array of opportunities for who I could become that following in the footsteps of your family wouldn't only seem archaic but kind of stupid? (Also,

---

15 Within my family obviously. I don't have the Sharansky kind of power.

16 It was my father's firm belief that to leave to build a new life at the age of 44 was basically akin to giving up your Moscow *propiska* and moving to a small town somewhere in the provinces. Which any respecting Moscovite would never do. Because a Moscow residency was worth more than all the caviar available on the black market plus a pair of Levi's and an original Bruce Springsteen record. Basically it was gold.

I learned that American medical education takes *11 years* and there was no way I was going to work with cadavers for *that* long.) In the land of freedom, the concept of freedom apparently didn't just apply to being free to purchase a used Nissan Sentra, or to go to a synagogue without a *kike* chorus screaming at you, or to buy as much *kielbasa* as you could. It also applied to being free to make your own decisions. Who would have thought?

Definitely not my parents. (Also not me—in the beginning, anyway.) But I know this now and I cannot stress it enough: immigrating and continuing to live someone else's dreams is a terrible idea. It's right up there with embalming a corpse and keeping it embalmed long after the regime that revered it is gone. But as a young immigrant I didn't really understand this and was pretty much consumed with two things: (1) how to please my family and (2) how to save enough money to buy a pair of Levi's as soon as possible. I managed to complete (2) within a few months but worked on (1) for years. But because I never became a doctor, or a lawyer, or an investment banker, or a real estate agent,[17] or a member of any trade that's brag-worthy in the Soviet-Jewish parent world, I was basically always set to fail. Which—having become a wise and mature person with jowls—brought me to a realization. Trying to make other people proud of you is as useless as trying to make a Russian literature teacher grade you at a 4 after you've disavowed Tolstoy. It's a lot easier to figure out how to be proud of yourself.

That's where the should-have-done-it bucket list comes in—and I'm here to tell you that with the help of that list, you too can be

---

17 This applies mainly to Sunny Isles Beach, Florida.

proud of yourself! Just look at me, finally studying what I want with zero guilt (and also using "esoteric" and "sangfroid" and even "perspicacious" in my Oxford essay while not plagiarizing forewords). Sure, I would have liked to do it when my brain was less shriveled, but *luchshe poszhe chem nikogda*,[18] right? And because it was Lenin who said "*Uchit'sya, uchit'sa y uchitsa*" (which basically means "Study, study, and study or else" in Soviet)—the statement that's been imprinted on my retinas ever since I was able to say mama[19]— my parents could feel assured that even while studying writing, I'm somehow following in their footsteps. Which actually bodes well for me when it comes to their wills.

My husband says I wanted to go to Oxford just to show off, but that's not *entirely* true. I also wanted to show my daughter that she too can do what she wants—whenever. And that the sky is the limit. And that she should follow her dreams. And that her mother is now an evolved parent who won't ever kill those dreams (even if they might lead right to the potential unemployment, heartache, and disillusionment of being a musical theater actress).[20]

---

18 "Better late than never," a slogan that was born either in a line for toilet paper or when Khrushchev finally spoke out against Stalin.

19 I remember it better than any quote by Shakespeare or Yeats or some other famous writer I'm supposed to cite *with ease* as an Oxford student. Please don't tell my tutors.

20 She's a very talented singer and has a voice of an angel—a cliché, I know, but I cannot think of anything better with my shriveled brain—so if you're in that industry, please hire her.

Which brings me to this monumental conclusion. I'm an evolved parent precisely because I ended up having to write the should-have-done-it bucket list. My Soviet childhood has been directly responsible for me winning at parenting and that's big. Also, if it weren't for that repressed bitterness I still harbor towards my upbringing, I wouldn't have had any material for this essay. And I wouldn't have written essays for *The New York Times*, *The Washington Post*, *The Guardian*, and *The Atlantic*.[21] Without which I probably wouldn't be at Oxford.

I guess what I'm really trying to say is that overbearing Soviet upbringing did me a lot of good. Right?

---

21 Last brag, I swear.

SOCIAL MEDIA—IS IT WORTH IT?

I didn't use to credit social media with much except for cute pet Instagram accounts, a chance to argue on Twitter with a Russian troll while @-ing Trump, and an occasional Facebook memory that doesn't make me grind my teeth wondering why on earth I ever posted *that*. Recently, though, I realized I owed the social media phenomenon more thanks than I thought. I'm going to get all philosophical on you now, but hear me out. Heraclitus, who lived way before the advent of texting thumb, apparently said something along the following lines: "No man ever steps in the same river twice, for it's not the same river and he's not the same man." Ignoring the sexism of christening all of humanity with the same gender, I'm going to go ahead and re-work this a little bit to apply it to friendship. As in, "You can never step into the same friendship twice, because it might be the same friendship and the same you, but it's sure as hell not the same friend."

I came up with this because of Facebook.[1] Unlike Twitter, where I go for professional reasons (a.k.a. checking how many times my writing has been shared by others, unfavorably compar-

---

1 If social media had been invented by the time Heraclitus came up with his philosophical utterances, he might have actually added Zuckerberg's name to the acknowledgments or whatever that section of papyrus rolls was called back in Ancient Greece.

ing myself with other writers, and occasionally tweeting snarky replies at politicians I disagree with) or Instagram, where I go to see what my daughter is up to (not anymore because it turns out there's something called Finsta, and Finsta is reserved for the selected few and I, the woman who carried her for nine months, birthed her for 24 hours, and tolerated her teenage antics for a thousand years, am not part of those selected few—please shoot me), Facebook is where I go to find out what happens in my friends' lives. Which is why I only friend people I meet in real life, and only keep them if I care enough to know about their kid's budding artistic talents or their dog's Halloween outfit or their 746th trip to Disney World.

While I Marie Kondo-ed the hell out of most belongings that didn't bring me joy way before Marie Kondo was a thing (or maybe even before she was born), there were always things—and people—I found hard to let go of. An old telephone book with the handwritten numbers of my school friends—even those who never invited me to parties; a little lacquer box a boy I liked gave me (probably his way of saying he wasn't going to ask me out on a date *ever*); a plastic Kermit the Frog I stole from my parents' friends' child in Moscow (because never in my life had I had a foreign, non-Soviet toy and why should other children have all the fun); my old, bifocal glasses that purported to cure myopia but made my face look like a Picasso-wannabe masterpiece; and a couple of friends I grew up with in Moscow who are now living in the US. I've kept these things because childhood nostalgia is real, even if you spent your childhood in the Soviet Union without Kermit the

Frog. And I've kept these friends because you need someone in your life to remind you of how far you've come from that needy teen who spent all of her waking hours comparing herself to others and won in that self-esteem bolstering contest never.

Here's is a thematic inside look at my friendship experiences, fueled by teenage angst and cemented in the trenches of coming of age in 1980s Soviet Moscow:

BFF FRIENDSHIPS

ME: Hi, can I speak to [redacted]?

A FRIEND'S PARENT: [Redacted] isn't here.

ME [wondering where she is because I'm sitting at home bored and she's most likely somewhere else having fun and why didn't she invite me?]: Can you ask her to call when she's back?

A FRIEND'S PARENT: Of course.

One hour later.

Two hours later.

Three hours later.

Four hours later.

Evening.

ME: Hi, can I speak to [redacted]?

A FRIEND'S PARENT: I'm sorry she's still not back.

ME [hyperventilating because it's obvious she is at some kind of party I was never invited to and she didn't bother to bring me along and why does my life suck so much]: Thank you.

CLOTHES

ME [chest inflated but voice nonchalant]: Hey, my dad just came back from [insert Warsaw-Pact country], you want to come over? [Surveying the loot my father brought me which I've been carefully laying out on my bed every morning so I can stare at them all day long only to have to move them at night because I have to sleep somewhere.]

Five minutes later.

A FRIEND: Wow, this sweater is gorgeous.

ME [glowing like a Kremlin star but only on the inside because I don't want to make her feel bad that she doesn't have a father who travels abroad and returns with foreign clothes]: I know. I'm wearing it to school tomorrow.

Rinse and repeat until one of my classmates jinxed me and the KGB demoted my father.

DATING

ME [sitting by myself at a party and jealously surveying a living room full of couples dancing so close to each other their teenage pheromones are already copulating]: ...

A FRIEND [back from dancing with her boyfriend]: My boyfriend said [redacted] likes you.

ME [feigning zero interest while trying to contain my suddenly racing heart within my chest cavity]: Him? Really?

A FRIEND [peering closer at me]: Wait, do you like him?

ME: NO!

A week later.

ME: [Redacted] gave me one ticket to *Yunona y Avos!*[2] He must have kept one for himself, right?

A FRIEND: Are you going?

ME: Of course!

A FRIEND: I knew it! You like him.

ME: I DO NOT, stop inventing things, it's *Yunona y Avos—that's* why I'm going! [Spend the next two weeks feverishly sewing a new outfit from a recent *BurdaModen* issue and daydreaming about sitting next to a boy who likes me enough to procure tickets to the Soviet equivalent of *Hamilton*.]

Two weeks later.

ME [dying a slow and painful death because love was never real for me]: [Redacted] called to offer me the second ticket because he says he can't go. You want to come?

A FRIEND: My boyfriend's taking me.

VACATIONS

A FRIEND [glowing like a decorated Stakhanovite]: My parents are taking me to [pick one: (1) a spa for the selected few, and by selected few I mean the crème de la crème of Soviet *apparatchiks* and their closest friends; or (2) downhill skiing, also known as that exclusive holiday no one in the Soviet Union has even heard of, much less went on]. What about you?

---

2 One of the hottest engagements in 1980s Moscow, also known as a sappy love musical especially adored by lovesick teens who needed confirmation that love was real.

ME [why does my life suck so much?]: My grandparents' summer house outside Moscow.

*

If these vignettes betray one fundamental truth about my coming of age in the Brezhnev/Andropov/Chernenko/Gorbachev USSR, it would be that it was spent in the thick, barbed-wire mound of competition. The *showing-off* competition. Which was very much in line with the rest of the country, except our focus was on kids' stuff and, namely:

- whether the boys you liked seemed to like you back
- how many of those boys there were in total
- how many of them wanted to marry you
- whether you had a boyfriend
- what kind of family that boyfriend came from
- what kind of family you came from
- whether it was the PhD-touting, exclusive-spa-access, down-hill-skiing-equipment-owning strata of the intelligenzia
- whether it was the occasional-Eastern-Bloc-business-trips strata of the intelligenzia
- whether it was the strata that didn't boast any of the above but still qualified for intelligenzia status
- whether your father drove a Volga, a Zhiguli, a Moskvich, or a Zaporozhets (God forbid)
- if it was a Zhiguli, whether he drove model #5 because that's the one that looked *most* foreign and required the levels of *blat* that may or may not have included Politburo members

- whether your parents' *blat* included Politburo members, Bolshoi directors, and university admissions officers
- whether all of the above made you cool enough to be invited to parties
- whether all of the above meant you had a pair of Yugoslav-made jeans to wear to those parties
- whether it was your own pair of jeans.

Because those showing-off competitions were almost always not in my favor, it'll come as no surprise that when I became the first in my circle of friends to move to the US I thought, "Ha! Now I'll show them." I spent the first few years in America writing them letters in which I inevitably mentioned my very own car (a used, no-defrost-in-the-winter Ford Escort but hey, it was *foreign* and also the equivalent of the latest Mercedes model in the quickly deteriorating Soviet Union-Russia of the 1990s), my several pairs of jeans, and the number of parties I was attending every week. Then some of my friends also moved to the US and showing off had to take on new heights, but I still felt like I had it under control with that uber-exclusive Ivy League degree, a diplomat for a husband, and a child who was trilingual and also adorable. Besides, most of that showing off was happening via an occasional email or a MagicJack phone call (remember those?) as I traversed the world in my too-cool-now-for-Levi's 7 for All Mankind bootcuts, and don't tell me you've never exaggerated the number of stars in your vacation hotels or the lack of toddler meltdowns during said vacations.

Then we decided to organize a reunion and you all know what that means, right? In normal (and by that I mean non-immigrant) childhood friends' reunions your intentions are probably: (1) to find out what their life has been like and (2) to compare it against your own while internally celebrating that you've done better than maybe 50 percent of your high school friends, and that the popular kids who used to throw your books on the floor are now living with their parents. All of this gets a lot more serious in the immigrant-childhood-friends get-together scenarios, because you are basically doing (2) while being completely conscious of the fact that your accomplishments in a country where neither the sky nor the furthest black hole is the limit are really not that great when compared with theirs, and that you may as well just take out a second mortgage so you too can buy yourself a BMW SUV. And then it gets even more serious, because you go to that reunion to desperately try to prove to yourself that you are an evolved human being who no longer needs to show off or impress anyone or make up for all the times you've felt inferior, and here you are telling your husband that you want that new German car only because it has heated seats.

Anyway, we got together on one of those beautiful summer after-noons when your shirt doesn't stick to your back with the sweat you accumulated while walking to the restaurant, and your hair doesn't frizz into an unmanageable mount of poorly-defined curls that want to eat your pasta primavera more than you do. My daughter and I arrived late and, since we had already eaten, we ordered a salad to share and an iced tea for her and sangria for me. The rest of the table ordered starters, salads, main dishes, desserts, and OYSTERS. Which—and please don't hate me for what I'm about to say—is the definition of a show-off food. I mean, who in their right mind would slurp down a ten-dollar mollusk, which tastes like rotten seaweed that washed up on the beach after floating through an ocean filled with plastic and human waste? Answer: no one. Another answer: your immigrant-childhood-friends who are trying to show off their expensive tastes.

Which was totally fine as long as I knew what they were up to and didn't have to subsidize that expensive taste. But then the bill came and the friend who ordered oysters suggested we split it and I heard that my share came to just under $100 *before the tip*. In case the dead mollusks distracted you enough to forget, that was for one salad, an iced tea and a glass of sangria.

Right, okay, I'll admit that our salad was great—locally grown, sourced, and whispered-to—but there were no truffles involved and we weren't eating at the Mandarin Oriental. The sangria, too, although delicious and made with real berries, didn't come with five Michelin stars, gold dust, and elfin tears from grinding that dust. And the ice tea was of a regular, unsweetened variety that my daughter wrinkled her nose at because sugar could never dissolve in a glass so stuffed with ice that tea was really an afterthought.

When my friend suggested we split the bill, my first thought was "WTF?" My second thought was "Holy shit, she's actually serious." I mean, don't get me wrong, I know people split checks all the time—something about math being a problem, although my phone can count just fine, can't yours?—and there are those who like to take advantage. Sitcoms have been filmed about this and George Costanza even complained about it on *Seinfeld* (I think?). Which is why my third thought was, "Should I say something and will that make me George?" (I didn't want to be George. No one wants to be George. Jerry—maybe. Elaine—definitely. Kramer—depends. But George? Definitely not.)

Still, at the risk of being George and also being uncool in the Soviet you-aren't-being-invited-to-that-party way, I raised the subject and said something about splitting the check according to what we all ate. But I either said it too quietly or they ignored me, or the idea of having their oyster habit subsidized was too vociferous. This left me no recourse but to swallow my non-existent self-respect (along with the last drops of sangria I wasn't leaving in my glass for that price), pay the $100 plus tip, and lie down right there as the doormat I still apparently was.

Here are a few thoughts that went through my mind as we said farewell and took a picture for either posterity or Facebook (or both because they're the same thing, right?):

- Oysters are the new downhill skiing.
- I need to learn to like them if I'm ever to win a show-off contest; a BMW SUV alone won't do it.
- Unless I do a better one and order lobsters smeared in caviar and bathed in Dom Perignon next time we get together.
- The evolved me isn't really that evolved, is it?

After that reunion, I decided that the only way for me to keep evolving while not reacting to my friends' show-off displays by mounting larger and better displays of my own was to just keep in touch via social media. That "unfollow" button is genius for never having to see videos of their dog's perfect performance at the Westminster Dog

188

Show or their attempts at mastering Scottish history as they explore "Lallybroch" on their private Outlander tour. And you, my friends, could also go ahead and do the same for me. Because, truth be told, I'm definitely guilty of posting my child's singing achievements every time she uploads a video to Instagram. This way we could all stay friends until Facebook explodes, which probably won't happen in our lifetime and, thus, as far as we are concerned, forever.

I believed that for a while, unfollowing people here and there, enjoying my unfettered-by-Soviet-habits online existence, and patting myself on the back for winning at friendships by keeping them oyster- and competition-free. But then one of my childhood immigrant friends decided to express her views on the 2016 election, the consequent Trump presidency, and the 2020/21 election/insurrection/impeachment/Senate acquittal/Trump 2.0, which isn't over quite just yet because Trump continues to stir up shit or what he calls "winning at losing."

Here I need to mention something you might not be aware of: lots of Russian immigrants voted for Trump in 2016 and probably voted for him again in 2020. This is because tax oppression is apparently real in this country, where we pay taxes at lower levels than most progressive countries, but also because they equate the Democratic Party with Brezhnev and who wants another go at those eyebrows? But, seriously, most Russian émigrés scream in all CAPS on their Facebook pages that socialism is coming and that socialism always means a Soviet-style hellhole with regular lines for butter, and not what most countries have in Europe with universal health care and not a day spent worrying about medical bankruptcies.

As far as I'm concerned, getting into arguments on Facebook is useless with just about anyone, but it's even more useless with former Soviets. Mostly because I'm no match for Fox News propaganda, but also because I'd have to do it in Russian and I refuse to spend 16 hours a day deciphering an argument written in convoluted sentences because that supposedly shows off (!) erudition. Half the time I have no idea what they're talking about and, honestly, I'd like to keep it this way.

Which is why instead of debating with that friend, I did the next best thing. Nope, not "unfriend and block" but hate-read every post and delight in the knowledge that, while I may not have that expensive oyster habit to show off, I'm definitely going to end up on the right side of history. And by that I mean, among people who didn't storm the Capitol and also people who know how to use CAPS sparingly. I'll be one of those few former Soviets who stayed progressive like they were back in the old country, even if they ended up upping their showing-off game with oysters, BMW SUVs, and philosophy quotes. Because you have to admit, there's some deep thinking in "You can never step into the same friendship twice, because it might be the same friendship and the same you, but it's sure as hell not the same friend" and, until now, philosophy was never something I was able to show off about. So, I guess, thank you Facebook for exposing the true colors of some of my "friends" and also for giving me a new hobby?

WATER WITH DINNER?
POUR ME ANOTHER GLASS

This may turn out to be one of those historical tidbits that never make it into the history books (and for that you are welcome), but Soviet people didn't drink water with meals. And by water I don't mean the fancy, bottled Georgian Borjomi you had to possess serious *blat* to procure, but regular, infused-with-the-best-heavy-metals-left-over-after-the-latest-five-year-plan water that hissed out of your kitchen faucet, sometimes clear and sometimes tinted just a little bit brown. Instead, we washed down our herring or *pelmeni* or buckwheat with hot black tea or with *kompot*, a drink concocted of boiling together whatever fruit you had on hand while adding enough sugar to dull the senses and forget that you'd just spent a combined five hours in two lines to get the fruit and the sugar. *Kompot*, or tea, or preferably both, was what we were expecting as we readied for the first meal we didn't have to make ourselves while in immigration.

Because, unlike in Vienna, our accommodations in Rome lacked kitchen facilities, all émigrés were given a full-board option for the first seven days we had to stay there. That first night we came down to the dining room in the basement hungry and giddy with excitement. Partially because we'd arrived on a train from hell early that morning and hadn't yet had a hot meal, but mostly because this would have been our very first *foreign* fare. Another historical tidbit I feel obliged to throw in here—although this one has probably already made it into a few history books—is that the vast majority of regular Soviet citizens had never traveled abroad (listen, they didn't call it the Iron Curtain lightly). If we define abroad as beyond the borders of the Politburo-tolerated Warsaw-Pact countries, it was an even vaster majority. And of those now stampeding with me down to that windowless dining basement, 99.9999 percent were part of this vast majority, and that's me being conservative. We were all Jews, and Jewish citizens of the Soviet Union weren't trustworthy enough to be allowed outside the USSR and live to tell about it.

Suffice to say we piled into that room like a herd of buffalos trying to get to the water source before it was all siphoned away for the benefit of just a few buffalos with appropriate *blat* connections. There were long tables with benches running along them and, okay, it looked like a gulag cafeteria, but at least the wood looked clean, polished, and didn't bear traces of any *vor v zakone*[1] knife carvings. We sat down, mouths and stomachs at the ready, when a side door opened and several young Italian men came out carrying stacks of metal bowls. They rushed along the tables, dropping those bowls in front of us, and, okay, this again was gulag-adjacent, but did they have such handsome serving staff in Siberia? I mean, sure, the sound of metal hitting the wood brought some unpleasant associations, even for those of us who hadn't experienced actual gulags, but I tried to concentrate on the positive by following those men with my eyes around the room until my mother elbowed me and handed me a handkerchief to wipe the drool off my chin.

---

1 Russian for "thieves in law" and Soviet-émigré for "that Leonov character in *Gentlemen of Fortune* that I still laugh at when I re-watch it decades later."

After a bowl was tossed in front of each émigré, two of the servers disappeared, soon returning with pots the actual size of Noah's Ark, which they balanced on their hips in their best imitation of Sophia Loren and her jug of wine in *More Than a Miracle*. They then proceeded to scoop—Olympic discus throw style—ladles-full of what looked like shortened *makaroni*[2] covered in red goo into our bowls. Here is an example of a conversation that ensued among the émigrés as this was happening:

"What is this?"

"*Makaroni*?"

"I can see it's *makaroni*, but what's it covered with? What's this red stuff?"

"I don't know. Looks like maybe tomato?"

"Tomato what? And who eats *makaroni* with tomato? Don't they have any butter or cheese?"

Meanwhile, as these indignant discussions filled the dining hall, the other two servers reappeared, carrying metal jugs. They placed them in strategic locations along the tables and this was the moment I called "here we go" and other émigrés called "WTF," which in Russian would be too crude to reproduce in exact translation. Here's how that conversation went in my family:

MY FATHER [of the metal jug glistening with condensation]: What is this?

---

2 Russian for pasta, which existed in the Soviet Union in only one shape and size—take spaghetti, marry it with wood logs, add grey food coloring, and serve with butter and cheese.

MY MOTHER [reaching out to the jug tentatively, pulling it towards her, and peeking inside]: Water.

MY FATHER: Hot water for tea?

MY MOTHER [touching the jug]: No, cold water. Ice cold.

MY FATHER [speechless]

THE REST OF THE TABLE WITHIN HEARING DISTANCE [speechless]

ME [pulling the jug towards me and pouring some water into my metal cup]

MY PARENTS [staring]: What are you doing? You'll get sick!

Another historical tidbit worth mentioning here is that in the Soviet Union there were no germs, and we mainly got sick because we drank or ate something cold (better eat that ice-cream at room temperature!) or because of drafty windows. But this wasn't the Soviet Union and there were no windows, so I decided to take my chances if this got me closer to *not ever being Soviet again*. The cold water felt strange in my mouth, but I swallowed it with the same pride pioneers feel when paving the way forward for others. Then I dug into my pasta and soon was shoveling it into my mouth especially enthusiastically because someone mentioned it wasn't properly cooked and someone else replied, "That's how they always make it in Italy. I read it somewhere, it's called *a denta* or something like that."

It was full-on assimilation into Western habits for me after that, and once we landed in America this included foregoing any and all Russian food. Before my parents and my grandfather moved away this wasn't easy, because my mother continued to cook for the family and I didn't think it was my place to deprive her of the task she'd done so well over the years. Plus, I would have felt bad robbing my grandfather of the potato-peeling responsibilities he'd grown accustomed to. Still, I did what I could and part of that effort included keeping all of my new American friends the hell away from our apartment, lest they discovered what my husband-to-be later called "lab experiments" and bizarre food combinations (like pancakes served with sour cream but without the caviar) my family consumed on a regular basis. Unfortunately, one time I let my guard down and Keith, who I wasn't dating yet but who I still wanted to impress with my most-assimilated-immigrant-in-the-history-of-all-immigrants status, walked in to discover a cheese cloth hanging off of the cabinet and dripping white liquid into the sink below.

"What's that?" he asked, wrinkling his nose in the way one would when visiting an outdoor, fifteenth-century latrine.

"*Tvorog*," my *dedushka* proudly declared. "I made it myself."

And before I could do anything to whisk Keith out of there or drop through the floor from embarrassment or at least prevent *dedushka* from sharing his pride and joy of the soured-milk-variety, my grandfather reached out for the bundle, took it down, untied the knot, and scooped a little bit onto a plate. "Here," he said, handing the plate to Keith, "try it."

"Put some sugar on it," my mother suggested, handing him a sugar bowl.

I wish iPhones were our addiction back in the year of our Lord 1990, because filming Keith's face would have probably netted me enough money on YouTube to out-earn "Charlie bit my finger" and "David after dentist" combined. Keith looked especially pained as my grandfather generously shared his recipe for this Russian-style cottage cheese. "I usually take a carton of milk," *dedushka* said, "leave it on the counter for a few days to sour, then pour it into this cheese cloth, and hang it over the sink for a few days. I did this in Moscow all the time."

I guessed that in Keith's household spoiled-on-the-counter milk was usually destined for the trash, not consumption, so I rushed to save him by saying he didn't have to eat it if he didn't want to. But my *dedushka* looked so excited to share his culinary talents that Keith forgot the entire germ theory and probably some of his common sense. He generously sprinkled the white mound of irregular and possibly e-coli-laced curds with sugar and ate a spoonful. At which point his whole body convulsed and he fell down with a trickle of the foamy, noxious substance seeping out of his mouth, and we had to conduct the first-of-many secret funerals of Americans we poisoned with Russian food.

Just kidding.

Keith survived, my grandfather survived (and made a few more batches, all the while lamenting the poor quality of American antibiotic- and hormone-infused milk which didn't make as good a *tvorog* as heavy-metals-infused Soviet milk), and I survived the embarrassment of having an American friend witness how very un-American I still was. The good news though was that Keith wasn't your run-of-the-mill local whose eyes usually glazed over whenever anyone mentioned anything that hailed from outside the continental US and had—God forbid!—a foreign name.

Once my parents moved away and my *dedushka* escaped to Los Angeles, where *tvorog* was as plentiful in Russian grocery stores as the number of immigrants who made selling your aunt's home-made Russian food at Neiman Marcus mark-ups a solid business idea, I immediately turned to frozen, ready-to-fry, supermarket French fries as my main food group. I supplemented that with an occasional discount pizza from Pizza Hut, a fish sandwich from Burger King, and—later at university after I'd become a vegetarian who occasionally ate Au Bon Pain's smoked turkey sandwiches because it was all right just once in a while—tortilla chips with salsa, consumed while standing up and accompanied by a bean salad with feta cheese, tomato, onion, and cilantro. Cilantro was the only ingredient in there, and in the rest of my American/whatever diet, that betrayed my Russian roots, but, listen, there will always be some things that are hard to give up.

My mother tried to lure me back to the mothership by preparing a spread of Russian *zakuski* every time I visited my parents, first in Ohio and then in Virginia where they moved. In response, I behaved like a complete asshole, and you'll understand why I'm saying this after I explain to you what *zakuski* are and why appreciating someone making them for you should be enshrined in the Russian constitution.

ZAKUSKI, AN OVERVIEW

Zakuski is Russian for appetizers, and any-Russian-home-cook for "how many platters can I fit onto this table while also (1) leaving enough space for guests' plates, silverware, and glasses; (2) inserting a respectable number of cognac and vodka bottles in between; and (3) in the process winning the title of Best Hostess With the Most Food Served in The History of Meals." The latter was a difficult award to attain and, therefore, in the days and centuries preceding said dinner, all female inhabitants of the 345-square foot apartment were expected to pitch in, and by pitch in I mean spend three-quarters of their lives making the *zakuski*. Which, when you hear what's involved, isn't going to seem an exaggeration at all.

THE KINDS OF *ZAKUSKI*

- The *Olivi'e* salad. Usually known to any Russian cook as the king of *zakuski* and also sometimes known as "Russian potato salad" among Americans or "*Ensaladilla Rusa*" among Spaniards and/or probably as [insert name of a potato-mayonnaise dish] in some other country. However—and I cannot emphasize this enough—comparing *Olivi'e* to any of the above can result in significant bodily injury if done within earshot of a Russian. And they'd be right to be offended, because as your resident Russian with years of experience of making *Olivi'e* I'm here to tell you that its recipe *isn't* just roughly chopped potatoes slathered in mayonnaise you bought at Costco. Instead, it's a carefully curated and impeccably arranged concoction of: diced boiled potatoes, diced boiled carrots, canned green peas, chopped fresh apple, chopped pickles, chopped hard-boiled egg, and chopped chicken or ham or some other animal flesh (if that's your jam). You spend a year-and-a half dicing and/or chopping all of the above and—I kid you not—I once drew a 1 cm x 1 cm square on a napkin as a size prototype so that my husband understood to which measurements he needed to pare down his Mount-Everestsized chunks of potato to pass my mother's inspection and to make it into her *Olivi'e*. After generously dressing all of the above with mayonnaise, you serve the salad in a crystal bowl and use your best Kandinsky impression to decorate it by arranging sliced boiled carrots around a twig of pastry you drive into the salad mound's top.

- Carrot salad. Made by grating fresh carrots and mixing this with pressed garlic, mayonnaise, and—if you don't live in my house and have to deal with raisin haters—raisins.

- Beet salad. Repeat the carrot salad instructions but instead of carrots use cooked beets and add chopped walnuts.

- (Have you had enough mayonnaise yet?)

- Deviled eggs. Boil some eggs, scoop out the yolks, mix with caramelized onion, shredded cheese of your choosing, and *more* mayonnaise, then stuff the egg-white shells with that concoction and serve on a platter decorated, once again, with that Kandinsky impression you mastered while making the *Olivi'e*.

- *Selyodka pod shuboi*. Translated as "herring in a fur coat" and made with layers of boiled potatoes, beets, and hard-boiled eggs—all mixed with plenty of mayonnaise—and plopped on top of a layer of herring.

- Cheese salad. Basically, grated cheese mixed with chopped garlic and mayonnaise—so don't forget a trip to Costco halfway through this culinary endeavor because by now you're running out of mayonnaise.

- Fish salad, in which you mix canned fish with chopped boiled eggs, rice, and onion, and dress it with mayonnaise.

- (Yes, now you've had enough mayonnaise.)
- *Kholodetz*. An aspic dish with meat and boiled eggs that would inevitably make me want to dry heave, which was the reason I never touched this stuff in childhood and, despite my family's protestations, it became the only Russian dish I never ate.
- *Vinegret* salad. Basically, a cousin of *Olivi'e* above, but with beets as the main ingredient. You dress it with oil and salt and it makes for a good *Olivi'e* substitute if Costco runs out of mayonnaise.
- Tomato, cucumber, onion, dill salad dressed either with oil or sour cream (there are two schools of thought on that one and you won't catch me taking a side), and salt.
- Sauerkraut of your own creation if you're living in the Soviet Union circa 1950–89, from a Russian grocery store if you're living in any Russian diaspora community that's big enough to have a Russian grocery store within a 30-mile radius, or the German kind from any American or other supermarket if you're not as lucky as the above.
- Pickles, pickled tomatoes, pickled anything that a Russian grocery store has on offer, or your regular American pickles, which are never the same but will do, because without pickles vodka doesn't burn your throat effectively enough to enjoy it.
- A platter of sliced cold cuts.
- A platter of sliced cheese.
- A platter of smoked salmon or some other smoked fish.
- Red caviar.
- Black caviar if you're really bragging.

My mother didn't make all of those when I came to visit, but she made quite a few. Which I almost always thanked her for by turning my nose up at those dishes, carefully prepared with bleeding knuckles, because I was too American to continue to ingest these amounts of mayonnaise and/or Russian food. And if that didn't make me enough of an asshole, then you'd be relieved to know that I drove that nail in deeper when I lectured her on using plastic wrap as she put away the leftovers of platters I barely touched. Plastic wrap was an American novelty to a former *Homo Sovieticus*, because in the Soviet Union plastic was the most desirable material after gold and also because if dishes were kept in the refrigerator anyway, why in the world did anyone need to cover them? But since I was living as a fully assimilated American, and Americans covered everything in Saran wrap, I felt it was my duty to inform my parents of the latest developments in germ theory and, in the process, assimilate them so that they wouldn't cause any undue embarrassment when and if I ever brought real Americans home.

With time my mother stopped making *zakuski* for my visits, and who could blame her? Then, when my daughter turned out to be much less of an asshole—actually, not an asshole at all—and showed my mother that she very much appreciated her efforts and also loved anything with mayonnaise, my mother started making *zakuski* again. She even taught her granddaughter the skill and they made *zakuski* together, soon expanding into hot dishes and even baking. I found their cookery scenes an adorable slice of a grandmother–granddaughter relationship and promptly recorded one of their sessions for an Instagram story while writing an article about them cooking together for another now-defunct food publication.

I credit my mother with showing my daughter that if the only food items in your fridge are eggs, onions, cheese, and mayonnaise, then an omelet isn't your only option and deviled eggs Russian-style would make for a respectable, albeit labor-intensive, replacement. I credit my daughter for never turning her nose up at her *babushka*'s cooking and for shaking me out of my self-induced reverie of assimilation snobbery. Sure, I still rarely (read: almost never) make *zakuski* at home and always decline food with mayonnaise (unless made by my mother—I've learned!) but I've relaxed enough in my identity as *still an immigrant* to stand next to my child as we make *lenivie vareniki*[3] or *blini*[4]—or, most of the time, to make it alone because she's rarely awake before noon. I figure that, despite this newly embraced softness towards my former Soviet eating habits, I can continue to claim the title of the most-fully-assimilated-Soviet-immigrant, because my Costco shopping list never includes mayonnaise and because tap water is still my preferred drink with any meal.

---

3 Kind of like gnocchi but made with *tvorog* (now available in any Russian grocery store and industrially produced and/or shipped from Mother Russia) and served with sour cream and sugar.

4 Russian crepes and my all-time-preferred breakfast food.

I FEEL BAD ABOUT THE BACK OF MY HEAD

First rule of parenting: do not pass your appearance obsessions on to your child. My mother wasn't careful and now I agonize about my thin hair, about my slightly-knock-knees (which look as removed from any idea of Russian beauty as Putin's nipples from the idea of sexiness), and about the flatness of the back of my head. The latter is the last thing I check before I leave the house. Because the way my occiput looks is more crucial than having keys, or wallet, or a phone.

Back in the old country we used to call those obsessions *komplexes*, as in—you guessed correctly—complexes; and if someone described you as someone with *komplexes*, it was one of the least complimentary things they could have said about you. Most of the time the sentences uttered were: "*U nee est' mnogo komplexov*" or "*Ona ochen' zakomplexovana*," both meaning "She has a lot of complexes." So right there you can clearly appreciate two things: (1) having complexes was almost always a female issue and, in fact, I don't think I'd be veering too much from the truth if I tell you that I don't remember a single time when that sentence referred to a man; and (2) the richness of the Russian language which boasts so many different conjugations, phrasal verbs, and clauses to demean a woman.

Here is the incomplete list of my complexes (incomplete because we'd need a lot more space for the complete list and my publisher told me this essay collection had to be a standard length).

LEGS

I never had or even aspired to have the kind of legs you'd attribute to high-cheekboned Russian beauties. I'm not that delirious. There weren't any genes in my family that would mislead me into thinking I could apply to a Moscow beauty competition and somehow advance past the measuring of the circumference of your thighs stage, during which the guy with the measuring tape would smirk at the extra centimeters and I would stand there in my Soviet-issue bathing suit and try to look dignified. But at the very least, I thought, my parents could have gifted me legs that didn't look *iksom*, which is Russian for "knock-knees" and Soviet-coming-of-age-girl for "the worst possible problem you can have with your legs and still be standing."

Nogi iksom was hands down the most unfavorable shape of legs anyone could have—so much so that whenever I came across girls with bowlegs, I stared at them enviously, while secretly longing for a leg-exchange operation. As far as I was concerned, knock-knees rendered me completely incapable of looking good, and I can tell you with complete certainty that wearing the tiny, beach-volleyball size black shorts that were the gym uniform in our prudes-meet-communist-morality-matrons' society was almost as painful as going to Soviet dentists whose idea of novocaine was that they didn't have any. I never wore short skirts or anything as revealing as leggings. (Did they exist even? Asking for real because I blocked all pieces of clothing that wrapped your legs like sausage casings from my mind.) One time my grandfather gifted me what could safely be described as every Soviet-citizen-under-30's-dream-a-jar-of-black-caviar-could-buy: stonewashed jean overalls. The first time I put them on I immediately donned a long jacket over them because these new overalls of mine were of the skinny leg variety and you didn't need an advanced degree to see that my body wasn't the body they were meant to hug. I spent the next two years wearing them while hiding them, and here's where you need to pause to feel the despair I suffered as I concealed the only item in my closet that was worth showing off to my friends and fellow Moscow metro riders. Also pause to recognize and appreciate the length to which a Soviet girl would go to hide her *nogi iksom*.

But my legs didn't disappoint me just because they could stand in for the first independent variable in any algebraic expression—the true meaning of the word *iksom*, by the way—but also because I hated my calves. My mother warned me that an early infatuation with heels (early? What is early for a woman in Russia, five? *Note:* this will go over your head if you've never lived in Russia) would cause my calves to look like those of a *kul'turist*, Russian for a body-builder and Soviet-mother-of-a-girl-child for "an abomination for any body but especially a female body." I spent the rest of my teenage life checking out everyone else's calves and obsessing if wearing kitten heels to a dance at the age of 12 had doomed me for life. It was also during this painstaking study of the lower leg muscles of every girl and young woman walking in front of me that I discovered that calves came in various shapes and sizes and that mine weren't at all worthy of even an occasional display.

EYES

My eyes should never have given me any *komplexes* because if I'm being maybe just a little bit braggy, they are one of my best features.

But you'd never know that if you looked at any of the impromptu photos of my younger self. That's because in most of them I appear like I've just sat down in a dentist's chair and I'm wincing because I know what's coming. I squinted so much between the ages of 13 and 19 that I could have long ago contributed a large amount to my dermatologist's down payment on a yacht, a.k.a. the Botox fund. Near-sightedness—also known as myopia to adults and "four eyes" to kids in my school—was what knocked me down from the popular kids' level to the dork level where I very strongly felt I didn't belong. But I had thick *and* bifocal lenses, so the levels of pain incurred while wearing those while being a teen girl far outpaced the level of pain in any Soviet dental chair.

My *dedushka* was very proud of those lenses, though. It took him not one, not two, and not even three degrees of *blat* separation to procure them because they were the newly invented Soviet version of the future Lasik surgery. They claimed to cure myopia with one clean swoop, if by clean swoop you mean wearing them *every single time you were in class*. Believe me, there was no one more eager than me to finally be able to see if the boy I was approaching on the street was actually the same boy I was crushing on at that time, but there was no way I was putting that contraption on to make it happen if it meant I'd be wearing them while he sat across from me in class. Instead, I learned to recognize people by their gait and to read whatever was written on the blackboard by looking through a tiny slit made by joining the thumbs and index fingers of both hands together. If you think figuring out what that blackboard read was painful, imagine what this must have looked like to the classmates

I hoped to impress. And I still thought this was miles better than wearing those glasses.

BREASTS

In principle, I didn't have any problem with my breasts except for the fact that THEY CAME IN WAY TOO EARLY. Those budding embarrassments decided to start poking through my gym uniform—a thin white T-shirt—before anyone else's, thus cementing my belief that life was cruel and that pubescent boys would laugh at anything with the word boobs in it. I responded to this crisis by hunching my shoulders far enough forward to hide these treacherous body image landmines in an attempt to once and for all put an end to the infinite flow of smirks coming from girls who were still flat and, thus, probably endlessly jealous that, despite my rapidly growing BRCA repositories, I could still heave myself over a pommel horse without getting stuck.

My father wasn't in agreement with having the Hunchback of Notre Dame as his daughter, and because most *Homo Sovieticus* believed positive change could only be achieved via criticism and disparaging commentary, he got right on that hammer-and-sickled red express to Make-Fun-Of-Rita-For-Her-Own-Good town. He took to calling me *gorbatko*[1] every time he came across my hunched-over shape, which was basically every day, many times a day. And then, not to be outdone, he added another nickname

---

1 A word he made up by creating a noun out of the adjective that meant "hunchbacked."

to his arsenal of daughter-improvement tricks. *Geimorita* was his pride and joy because he invented it by combining two words—my name and the Russian term for a chronic sinus infection. He did this because in my early teens I suffered from recurring sinus infections, which annoyed him because I walked around with a stuffed nose and constantly sniffled. (*Note:* since antibiotics or whatever other humane methods existed in the world for curing this ailment hadn't yet made their appearance in the Soviet Union, I was hospitalized for a month, during which doctors punctured my sinuses with a thick needle and *without* anesthesia every day. That month concluded with them removing my adenoids, *also* without anesthesia.)

Because my hunched shoulders and my sniffling irritated my father's sensibilities equally, and because both nicknames started with the same letter and rolled off his tongue together as easily as a Pushkin poem, he called me both names at the same time. This went down in the history of our household as "harmless fun for a good cause" and in the history of my teenage angst as "how do I never cross paths with my father in this 345-square foot apartment?"

FACE

Until I was about 18 my face didn't give me any trouble. But then one day I was on my way home on the metro, partially reading a new *samizdat* novel and partially daydreaming about a vacation I was about to take with a friend to a Black Sea resort, when I felt something not quite right with my face. One half of it appeared weird and immobile, and suddenly I couldn't scowl in that typical Moscow fashion where you wanted people around you to know you hated humanity and especially them. One part of my face scowled just fine actually, but the other lagged behind. I came home and my mother immediately rushed me to our local polyclinic where a doctor with henna-dyed orange hair under her tall, starched white cap looked me over, and in reply to my anxious question about whether or not I could still go on my holiday, said, "Why not? Sea water would do you good."

It turned out she was wrong and instead of that holiday I ended up in a hospital for Bell's palsy (the Soviet health care system loved to hospitalize people when they least needed it). I spent a whole month there while envy-reading letters from my friend who went on that holiday with another friend. They both met cute guys and I was reading about their dances and late-night adventures while confined to a room with four beds, surrounded by doctors who wanted to inject medicine right into my ear, and working with a physical therapist who stuck his fat fingers into my mouth—*without* washing his hands first—because he wanted to prevent my cheek muscles from atrophying.

He didn't: they atrophied just fine. When I came home after that glorious summer month of *borscht*-aroma hallways, I was the new proud owner of a face that Picasso would have called "Cubism but amateur." My eyebrows didn't line up, half of my mouth didn't smile symmetrically with the other, and one of my eyes watered suddenly and at odd times, but also almost always when there was a boy I liked somewhere in the vicinity. Add to this that I was living the nightmare of almost every one of my friends dating a steady boyfriend-nearly-fiancé, while I didn't even have anyone who called my landline to either hang up or breathe loudly down the phone, and you have a fully made, Aristotle-approved dramatic structure for a coming-of-age-in-times-of-Soviet-health-care-excellence romcom.

Now that you've had a good fill of my youthful insecurities, let me come clean. I *still* have some of them (plus an assorted collection of others not described above). Some, because I've been very much into the personal growth (of the glow-up variety, partially!) industry for almost half of my mature-life years, which resulted in the following:

- Rushing to that Lasik surgery waiting room as soon as I was fairly convinced it wouldn't blind me. While inhaling the burned eyeball aroma and seeing nothing but black when the doctor lasered the shit out of my myopia terrified me more than a childhood trip to the mausoleum to gape at Lenin's decaying corpse, I still remember the feeling of waking up after my Xanax-induced stupor to see the alarm clock with perfect clarity and rejoicing with a vigor that only a Soviet Young Pioneer could at the exit from said mausoleum.

- Being diagnosed with BRCA-generated breast cancer and swapping my breasts for implants that would never bounce if I were now to jump over a pommel horse.

- Familiarizing myself with the wonders of Botox, hyaluronic acid, and photo rejuvenation to even out the wrinkles and eyebrows while simultaneously restoring my face to the glory of looking like the 18-year-old before the Bell's palsy. (As an aside, photo rejuvenation takes care of those sunspots you've acquired while trying to make up for that missed vacation by

sunbathing extensively during other vacations. The procedure involves a numbing cream you wish Soviet dentists had,
a laser zap,[2] and bursts of light bright enough to illuminate
all of your *komplexes*, past, present, and future.)

- Not jealously eyeing my mother's legs and wondering why the
hell I didn't take after her because her legs are straight, have
zero cellulite (how is it even fair that I have cellulite and she
doesn't?), and exhibit the kind of calves that any adolescent
Soviet girl would be proud of.

- Doing everything in my power not to pass on any of my
komplexes to my daughter—and begin that process by *never*
swaddling her because swaddling and leaving me on my back
for extended periods of time as an infant were single-handedly responsible for my flat head and the number of hours I've
wasted trying to puff my thin hair over it. (My daughter's head
is now perfectly round and not at all obsession-inducing.)

- Continuing that process by never mentioning any of my
remaining *komplexes* anywhere in my child's vicinity and by
never criticizing or making fun of her appearance.

I probably don't have to tell you that the last one was the hardest—
yes, even when compared to cancer, Lasik, and acid injected directly
into your face. Old habits die hard and sometimes not at all, and
really, how many plausible explanations could you provide when you
showed up at home with bruises around your marionette lines (not

2 I think it's a laser, but don't quote me on that. Always speak to your
doctor; this isn't a dermatologist-approved book.

at all a testimony of my dermatologist's skill—I just bruise easily) or looking like five Dalmatians merged into one? Harder still was not to comment on how she brushed her hair (come on, child, puff it up around the roots, especially at the back), how she walked with her toes pointing inward (a definite disgrace for a ballet-superpower-raised parent), and how she hunched her shoulders just like I did despite the absence of pommel horses in her gym class and the wide availability of all kinds of bras in her adolescent life.

I'm not here to claim that I'm a perfect mother, but, listen, I tried my best and I even once got into a fight with my parents when they criticized her posture. That wasn't pleasant, especially because the fight took place in the dining hall of the largest cruise ship in the world with a built-in audience of about 6,000 people. So that should count for something, right? I mean, I may still be the perfect target audience for volumizing shampoos and gels and sprays of unicorn dust, but at the very least the word *komplex* will die with me. My daughter can thank me for this later.

PS: *Reminder to self*—do *not* ask my daughter what the back of my head looks like ten times a day. Reduce the number of times to zero, or, if not possible, to one.

OLD HABITS DIE HARD

The other day my husband had to pack for a trip. And, because it was a short trip and he needed a small suitcase, he went rummaging through the closet in the guestroom where we keep the luggage. In the process of that rummaging he took out several other suitcases, a bag I didn't know we still had, and an old yoga mat I keep for sentimental reasons. He took them out, left them there with the closet doors still open, and went to pack in our bedroom. Or somewhere else. Honestly, I don't keep track of where he usually packs.

If you still can't guess where this is going, re-read the fourth sentence in the previous paragraph. Because at some point later I walked into that guestroom to get my laptop and tripped over the bag I didn't know we had. And then, in the process of trying to recover my balance without hitting the corner of the daybed, I saw the open closet and the yoga mat and the other suitcases scattered around the floor. My first thought was, "Why do we have so many red suitcases?" Then I realized we didn't and I was just seeing red. (I know it's an overused cliché and I realize it comes from bull fighting which I don't at all condone and that's why I'm going to try to edit that metaphor out in the next draft.)

After I avoided falling down, and after I confirmed that we weren't indeed the owners of three bright red suitcases, I marched directly into the kitchen and yelled at my husband. He was already there having his morning yogurt and evidently not at all worried about the commotion in the guestroom. The yelling went along these lines:

ME: Do you know what just happened?

HUSBAND [chewing loudly and staring at his phone]: Um? What?

ME: I JUST FELL.

HUSBAND [serving himself more yogurt, dripping some on the counter because he is *still* staring at his phone]: You did?

ME: Why is all this stuff out of the closet in the guestroom?

HUSBAND [suspecting where this is going—I know he suspects it because he's scooping his yogurt into his mouth more slowly; or maybe it just looks that way because I'm getting ready to pounce]: I was taking out my suitcase.

ME: I KNOW THIS. Why is the rest of the stuff still out?

HUSBAND: Relax. I'll put it back.

For the record, when my husband tells me to relax I definitely don't. Mostly because who can relax on command, and also because after years of tripping over shoes, suitcases and briefcases, and after two decades of picking his dirty laundry off the floor (to his credit, he learned to do it himself a few years ago), and after what seems like a millennium of finding cluttered kitchen counters *every time* he makes food, I don't have any relaxation left in me. I don't even have a reasonable volume voice. All I have left is yelling. Which he takes issue with.

HUSBAND: Why are you yelling?

ME [mostly trying to find my breath because I'm so angry I can see enough red for a new Russian Revolution]: WHY? [Really all I can squeeze out because I cannot understand how he doesn't grasp the severity of what's happened.]

HUSBAND [thinking he's grasping it and coming towards me to try to put his hands on my shoulders]

ME: DO. NOT. DO. THIS. DO. NOT. TOUCH. ME.

It's at times like these that I think he's actually completely clueless. And that leaving stuff around isn't malice but just him being him—a person who, even though we're past our silver wedding anniversary, still DOES NOT realize he can't diffuse my levels annoyance with a hug. (If you're reading this and condemning me because your two-decades-old annoyance is easily erased with a peck on the cheek, maybe you should stop reading. It gets messier.) So, if he doesn't understand that hugging me is strictly prohibited when I turn into a small-scale dragon, he definitely doesn't understand that if he leaves anything lying around it's eventually *me* who picks it up. There are no hard-working elves that come out at night and clean our house, I cannot stress this enough.

But the worst act of cluelessness happens after he goes into the guestroom and puts away the suitcases.

HUSBAND [after sounds of suitcases being stacked and closet doors being closed, while still in the guestroom]: Done. Happy now?

I think he says it from the guestroom because he can sense that what he is saying is problematic. And that the time it takes me to fly from the kitchen to the guestroom is enough for him to summon St. George. So, after thinking this over, maybe he isn't as clueless as he appears to be. Maybe it's *all* calculated.

The "Happy now?" question is loaded. It contains several meanings. Several questions, really. There is the one about me being happy that my guestroom is now free of obstacles, and that the suitcases and the bag and the yoga mat are back to where they belong. That's a definite yes. There is another one about me being happy that it's finally been done and that I didn't have to do it *myself* for a change; after some thinking, I'd say that's also a yes. And then there is the one which he clearly wants to convey, and that one goes something like this: "Are you happy that I have done this tiny little task that was so not worth yelling about and that you made a huge deal out of when it was so insignificant and why couldn't you do this yourself; it's *so not difficult*, especially as proven by the fact that it took me a total of 15 seconds to do it." The answer to this one is a definite no. Followed by another breath of fire (not the yogi kind).

So, in the spirit of a public service announcement and to help you avoid these and other unnecessary misunderstandings, here's a list of habits you might want to remember if your partner is a Soviet émigré:

AKKURATNOST', OR PLEASE PUT THINGS BACK WHERE THEY BELONG

After my husband left on his trip (LEAVING the yogurt container in the sink for me to take care of, obviously), I decided to attempt some personal growth. I wrote a WhatsApp message to two friends asking them whether I was justified in my annoyance or whether I was just too anal about these things. I asked them because I was thinking of writing an essay in which I could subtly complain about his leaving-shit-all-over-the-place habit. I thought about writing that essay because I once wrote an essay about how my hairbrush always went MIA whenever my teenage daughter used it. That essay was basically *akkurantost'*-adjacent and obviously two essays are better than one when you want to get your point across. Since you haven't read that first essay (and you won't since it's not in this collection) I'll save you the trouble and summarize it for you.

I'm USSR-born.

My husband is American-born.

We are raising a daughter.

When she becomes a teen, she starts taking my hairbrush and she *never* puts it back.

This is against the motto of *akkuratnost',* also known as *vzyal, polozhi na mesto,* which basically means "put things where they belong" in English and "you're gulag-bound if you don't" in Soviet. I taught her this motto when she was a toddler.

After this happens for the 1,015th time, I raise my voice.

My husband tells me I'm being anal and that I don't know how to share.

I start hiding my hairbrush.

She starts taking his and *never* puts it back.

He gets upset after the third time it goes missing and raises his voice. I rejoice (inside) and continue to hide my brush.

From the hairbrush, she goes on to borrowing his phone chargers, iPads, and headphones. She *never* puts them back.

I win. My hairbrush is *always* where I hid it (and so are my headphones and chargers). And I feel vindicated every time I say, "I told you so."

The end.

Akkuratnost' is the thread that connects the brush and the suitcases. I won't speak for the other former Soviet families out there, but in my family, *akkuratnost'* is second only to complete and total reverence towards your parents (to not revere your parents enough is to basically be the new Stalin; you don't need to be a historian to know how bad that would be). *Akkuratnost'* is Russian for being neat, Soviet for having a respectable upbringing, and Soviet woman for thank-God-and-my-mother-in-law-that-my-husband-at-least-knows-how-to-fold-his-clothes. Just ask my mom. My father still doesn't know how to turn on the stove. Or how to clean a bathroom. Or how to give any space to a woman's opinion. But he picks up after himself.

My mother says it's because he grew up *akkuratnym*. And that's because his father was also *akkuratni*. (Those are all conjugations of the word "neat", and if you don't think that's too many and that maybe one day you could master them all, I'm here to tell you *don't even try* because there are at least 300 more for this word alone.) In fact, my grandfather's *akkuratnost'* was so legendary that it cost him a few thousand roubles. That's because when my father's younger brother married and his new wife moved in with his parents, her levels of *akkuratnost'* were so not up to par with her new father-in-law's that they had a huge fight, and my grandparents had to buy the young couple a new apartment. Which was completely unheard of in the Soviet Union. You lived with your parents or your spouse's parents when you married; that was the rule of Soviet socialism. (*Note to historians and USSR lovers who will leave me nasty comments:* I know it was not the rule on the books. I'm not trying to rewrite history. But you go and find housing you could acquire or rent legally. Or any housing at all.)

Anyway, I thought my friends would confirm my righteousness and also dismiss the concern that I was anal. Which they kind of did—kind of because it didn't feel like a strong enough confirmation or a complete dismissal. But I think that was because they were mostly concerned that I write a balanced essay and not just spend 800+ words complaining about my husband (which, obviously, I can do easily as, for the record, this essay is already up to 1,700+). We went back and forth about the role that gender dynamics, generation, and culture might play in cleaning up after yourself but in the end reached no decisive conclusion, mainly because we aren't sociologists or anthropologists.

But in the course of that WhatsApp exchange we did discover what felt like some universal truths. *Felt* is the operative word here. We agreed that lots of people don't see their own mess (no conclusive statistical data on this but I think we are definitely on to something) and that it's more annoying seeing other people's mess. And I agreed that if there was anything to agree with, it was that my husband could be a *little* more Russian. Not in an embracing Putin kind of way, but in seeing his mess and dealing with it before I trip over it.

SMEKALKA OR *NAKHODCHIVOST'*, BUT BASICALLY UPCYCLE WHENEVER YOU CAN

My husband and I once stayed in a furnished apartment and their idea of a cutting board was "flexible cutting mats," which were just as removed from what a cutting board should be as any sharp knife should be from a cutting board *this* flexible. To be able to slice vegetables and not feel like we were skating on a lake that used to freeze just fine but now doesn't because of climate change, we went out and bought our own cutting board. And then I used these "cutting mats" as placemats. To be completely honest, this didn't require as much *smekalka* as I'd like to claim as a former Soviet—the word "mats" was already in the name. But I'm going to count that one as a win anyway because my husband was surprised. As in, he-would-never-have-thought-of-it surprised.

Smekalka is Russian for savvy and resourcefulness, modern Russian for *laifhak* (borrowed from—can you guess?), and Soviet for "extreme DIY." We adjusted, repaired, invented, and improved everything. To illustrate:

SHOES AND ESPECIALLY FOREIGN-MADE SHOES

A huge deficit item and, thus, a large source of pride for the entire family. So when your grandfather uses his contacts to get you a pair of Japanese-made Mary Janes to wear on the first day of school, you don't complain that they are a size too small. Instead, you spend several weeks prior to that monumental occasion of impressing your new classmates and teachers with the best footwear in a 2,000-mile radius walking around your apartment while wearing your new shoes with wet socks, because your neighbor has learned that crafty knack from reading the "Home tricks" section of *Science and Life* magazine. Also, because a famous comedian once said that having the wrong size of footwear wasn't a good enough reason not to wear that footwear, and if that's not a perfect metaphor for life in the USSR I don't know what is.

MITTENS

Nothing is easy to buy in the Soviet Union and mittens aren't an exception. To make sure your child returns home with both mittens still in their possession, sew each to the end of a long, wide elastic string and pass that string through the sleeves of your child's coat. There they remain until your child learns what being an embarrassing dork means, or until school bullies point it out—whichever comes first.

MAKE-UP

Make-up of any kind is synonymous with having it all while still clutching a bus pole in hopes of not falling onto your neighbor in a crowded vehicle as it hits pothole after pothole on a regular Moscow street. There's no such thing as an expiration date because that French mascara you paid someone for in Bolshoi tickets never expires, so you spit into it when it gets too hard. For the lipstick you bought after a three-hour queue when the miracle of "*ee vybrosili v GUMe*"[1] happens during your workday, you use a match to extract every last fragment because you aren't repurposing that plastic tube until every bit of color is gone from it.

PERIOD PARAPHERNALIA

I watched *The Queen's Gambit* the other day and in horror realized that in 1960s America they had menstrual pads. You know what

---

1 Russian for "it was thrown out at GUM," the main Moscow department store with the lowest product per square meters of shelf space density in the entire USSR, or Soviet for "this item has just appeared in GUM, hurry up, the line's already forming and, don't worry, the boss knows and is probably already there."

we had? If you were lucky: a gigantic wad of cotton you jammed into your privates, hoping nothing would leak through during the school day because there were no old newspapers to wrap it in, and who wants to be responsible for adding the metallic aroma of that exfoliating uterus to a bathroom that already smells worse than a medieval latrine? If you weren't lucky: a rag you used, washed, and re-used.

PRAVDA SUNSCREEN

Better to have a piece of the main national newspaper glued to your nose with saliva than a peeling nose when you come back from that vacation on the Black Sea.

PLASTIC BAGS

Washing out and drying that one plastic bag that came into your possession is not weird at all and everyone does it because we all know how valuable plastic bags are, especially if they have any kind of foreign writing on them. Rinse and repeat for as long as that foreign writing stays intact—you'll be a dude-magnet with it, regardless of how the rest of you looks.

Because throwing things out wasn't a Soviet concept, our soon-to-be-communist paradise was a zero-waste country before it was in vogue. Shops were mostly empty, and you literally couldn't have a bicycle if you didn't fashion one out of the old wheels you found at your grandparents' dacha. Also, you'd be surprised at how versatile old scraps of metal and rubber could be if you were living in a country where spare car parts were just as rare a sighting as a child without the elastic-string-held mittens.

None of this is something my American-born husband understands, and that's why this kind of dialogue happens in our house almost daily:

ME: Why is this shirt in the bin?

HUSBAND: It's missing a button.

ME: It's *what*?

HUSBAND [slightly louder]: It's missing a button.

ME: I heard you. I'm asking why a perfectly fine shirt is sitting here in this trash receptacle when it could be hanging in your closet?

And it's not always about shirts. It's also about broken suitcases that are perfectly fixable, about shoes whose only transgression are worn soles, and about sheets of paper that are *still* two-thirds unused. One time he wanted to discard a perfectly good suit because there was a rip in his pants' pocket. My husband throws out everything. I fish it back out of the trash.

But I'm not a hoarder. My actions are driven by the combination of *na vsyakij sluchai* and *vprok*, which—translated from Soviet—means "waste not, want not," or "just in case I need this sometime in the future to fix a carburetor in a car I don't yet own." When added to *smekalka* it means you too could contribute a creative solution to an everyday Soviet problem by sharing that hack you've discovered with the readers of the "Home tricks" section of *Science and Life* magazine.

Okay, so no, I don't fix cars and there are plenty of auto parts stores in the US. But, listen, that born-in-the-USSR bug is like herpes—you just can't get rid of it. It sits in your system and inflames every time someone in your household decides to throw out something you still consider usable. For example, my art studio is now full of broken cup fragments, tulle scraps, old CDs, and used chopsticks. You just never know when you're going to need that old zipper or when pieces from that broken stained-glass wind chime would fit seamlessly into a painting you're working on. For which, incidentally, you're using—instead of a canvas—several wine boxes you picked up on the street because it should be an Interpol crime to throw out perfect wooden boxes that could be re-used 567 ways and that's a conservative estimate based only on one YouTube craft video you've looked up.

All I'm saying is that all of those things would have been in a landfill right now. Instead, thanks to *smekalka*—now known as "upcycling" in my house—they're art. (Also, thanks to whoever coined the term upcycling, because I can now rescue things out of the trash and not feel ridiculous about it.)

VEZHLIVOST' AND *VOSPITANIE*, OR YOUR MOTHER-IN-LAW'S RULES ON HOW YOU MUST BEHAVE

These translate as politeness and upbringing and mean all of the following when coming out of the mouth of a Soviet émigré:

- To say hello, thank you, and please.
- To open the door for the elderly and women.
- To give up your seat on public transport for the elderly and women.
- To help the elderly and women carry heavy packages.

- To have read Tolstoy, Gogol, Dostoyevsky, Pushkin, Krylov, Turgenev, Bulgakov, Solzhenitsyn, Yesenin, and Mayakovsky, plus an occasional tome of Hemingway, Remarque, Dickens, and any other Western writer deemed safe enough by the Soviet censors to be translated into Russian.
- To quote Tolstoy, Gogol, Dostoyevsky, Pushkin, Krylov, Turgenev, Bulgakov, Solzhenitsyn, Yesenin, and Mayakovsky, plus an occasional tome of Hemingway, Remarque, Dickens, and any other Western writer deemed safe enough by the Soviet censors to be translated into Russian.
- To understand the deeper meanings of Tolstoy, Gogol, Dostoyevsky, Pushkin, Krylov, Turgenev, Bulgakov, Solzhenitsyn, Yesenin, and Mayakovsky, plus an occasional tome of Hemingway, Remarque, Dickens, and any other Western writer deemed safe enough by the Soviet censors to be translated into Russian.
- To recognize music by Tchaikovsky, Mussorgsky, Rachmaninoff, Mozart, Beethoven, Bach, Chopin, Brahms, Vivaldi, Stravinsky, and Verdi.
- To play piano and to be able to play music by Tchaikovsky, Mussorgsky, Rachmaninoff, Mozart, Beethoven, Bach, Chopin, Brahms, Vivaldi, Stravinsky, and Verdi.
- To understand the deeper meanings of music by Tchaikovsky, Mussorgsky, Rachmaninoff, Mozart, Beethoven, Bach, Chopin, Brahms, Vivaldi, Stravinsky, and Verdi.
- To have been to the theater.
- To have been to the opera.
- To have been to the ballet.

- To offer help in the kitchen when coming over as a guest for dinner. (*Note:* if you're Russian-born, living in the US, and are already aware of this rule, DON'T FOLLOW IT. You and I both understand we're just being polite and that we do *not* actually want to help. Americans don't understand this. They'll actually put you to work assembling a salad or dressing said salad with one of the 1,354 salad dressings they have in their fridge. I made the mistake of offering help right after I arrived in the US and now I know only to offer it in Russian households because—see below.)

- To refuse help in the kitchen when offered by a guest coming to dinner.

- To reciprocate a dinner invitation.

- To make your dinner just as elaborate as the dinner invitation you're reciprocating (see essay *Water with Dinner? Pour Me Another Glass* for menu suggestions).

- To never come to a Russian-born person's house empty-handed, whether for dinner or a visit. (*PS:* Seriously, *never ever* do this. Bring something. Flowers, chocolates, a bottle of wine, cognac or expensive vodka—don't skimp there, Russians know their vodka—toys for the kids, nicely wrapped French macaroons for dessert, ANYTHING. *PPS:* That anything should under no circumstances include any soap or spa products, even-numbered flower bouquets,[2] or a box of Ferrero Rocher, which you should have known has lost its

---

2 Those are strictly reserved for funerals. So whenever my husband gets me flowers, we always end up needing two vases because we split one

gourmet candy status with diaspora Russians ever since it
started selling in Walgreens and CVS. *PPPS:* call my family-
in-law and teach them this rule.)

- +549 more rules, but my publisher tells me I'm running out
  of space.

I know this seems like a lot and I'm not saying you need to learn all of
these words and concepts in one week. Or even in two. My husband
is still learning, some 1,043 weeks later, but he's made progress. For
example, he now always disposes of the used yogurt containers after
finishing his yogurt and, sometimes, he even offers them to me in
case I have a use for them. And it's been at least a month since I last
tripped over the shoes he leaves right in the middle of our hallway.
That's a lot of headway, so I'm going to overlook the fact that he still
hasn't read *Anna Karenina*. He can watch it on Netflix and, sure, it's
a cop-out but my parents don't need to know this if they ever decide
to discuss the deeper meanings of Levin's moral journey with him.

---

even-numbered bouquet into two odd-numbered ones. Which is,
obviously, okay with me because two bouquets are better than one.

IS THERE A RUSSIAN *BABUSHKA* INSIDE ME AND, IF SO, CAN I BE HELPED?

This is a recent conversation I had with a friend:

FRIEND: Do you remember you once came over for lunch with Eliana? She was tiny then.

ME [hoping the visit went well because tiny Eliana was adventurous and curious and in other people's houses that wasn't always a good thing]: I think so.

FRIEND: Do you remember I told her not to jump on my couches?

ME [Oh, God, here we go]: I don't. Did she break anything?

FRIEND: No, but do you remember what she said to me?

ME [shaking my head, terrified I was just as much into four-letter-words then as I'm now]: No?

FRIEND: She said I was just like a Russian *babushka*.

At this point you're probably wondering how old Eliana was and what exactly she meant by calling my friend a Russian *babushka*. Sadly, I HAVE NO IDEA. Because, apparently, my memory decided to forego retaining this adorable incident in which my daughter proved to be a wunderkind with an insight into people's characters in order to preserve a fully intact recollection of that time I ate a lukewarm microwave waffle with strawberry jelly during a morning break from a temp job I once had.

Anyway, back to the Russian *babushkas*. The conversation made me wonder: would I—obviously later in life because I'm definitely not ready to be a grandmother to anyone yet—concede to being called a Russian *babushka*? And enjoy the simile as much as my friend did? Had anyone asked me this when I was a child, grand-mothered by two of the best *babushkas* in the whole Soviet Union, I would have given a resounding yes. Had anyone asked me the same question after I had my own child and learned for the first time that when you cross a Russian *babushka* with US-style capitalism you get a made-in-America-Russian-*babushka*, I would have probably said no. For those of you asking me now, you'll have to wait until the end of this essay to get your answer because it's not simple, and also because I don't like spoilers.

If you'd grown up with Russian *babushkas,* you'd know what your child would be in for if they ended up having one in their lives. If you didn't grow up with Russian *babushkas*, you're in for a treat because I can prepare you for the minefield of peonies slash a really rich buffet of love mixed with guilt trips it'll be for you and your child. Behold.

RUSSIAN *BABUSHKAS* ALLOW THEIR GRANDCHILDREN DO ANYTHING THEY WANT—ANYTIME AND ANYWHERE

Unless anywhere means my parents' couches, on which my daughter probably tried to jump as a toddler, forcing my mother to re-exam-ine her dedication to being a real Russian *babushka* and resolving instead to become a made-in-America-Russian-*babushka*—a change of heart no one can blame her for. That's because when my mother decided to be your regular Russian *babushka*, all she had was her mother's example, and that example didn't include expensive, Italian-made couches. It also didn't include instances of anyone jumping on couches, because in the Soviet Union couches were never that comfortable or sturdy.

All of the above isn't to say that my mother doesn't know how to spoil her granddaughter. She's done such a great job of it, in fact, that I've heard my father repeat the same accusation he'd leveled at her parents in Moscow every time he and I had an argument that dissolved into screaming. "It's your parents, they've spoiled her rotten," he'd always say. Now he says the same thing about my mother spoiling my daughter, forgetting that he spoils her just as much—and by "just as much" I mean they go together to buy her a new phone whenever she asks for it. But at least he isn't there cooking her meals three times a day and slicing an apple for her and making her a cup of tea while she lies in bed engrossed in Netflix so, yeah, I guess he isn't spoiling her too much.

RUSSIAN *BABUSHKAS* FEED THEIR GRANDCHILDREN

That's "feed" typed in 48-point font and formatted in italics and CAPS while simultaneously being bolded and underlined. One of my grandmothers was so concerned about me having a hot lunch after getting home from school that she ignored her heart murmur and every day made a trip to our apartment to feed me. *Babushka* Betya lived a 20-minute walk away and, let me tell you, that walk included hills. While she climbed them, she had to stop every three minutes to catch her breath, and that's the kind of grandparenting dedication my mother aspires to as she stands in the kitchen three times a day preparing my daughter's favorite foods.

Don't get me wrong, I'm not against grandparents cooking for their grandchildren. One of my favorite dishes growing up was fried potatoes with onions and only if prepared by my *babushka* Betya. My other grandmother—*babushka* Olya, who lived a 36-hour train ride away—made the best eggplant caviar, a recipe I have never been able to replicate (I blame the subpar American tomatoes). And the memory of *babushka* Betya's New Year's Eve dish of apple-stuffed duck still activates my salivary glands even though I've not eaten poultry or meat for almost three decades and don't intend to start again.

But there's the idea of feeding your grandchild when they're hungry and it's time to eat, and there's my mother's idea of feeding her grandchild. Which is basically a 24/7 feeding schedule that's solely based on "look at her, she's all *zelenaya*." This translates as "green" in English and as "unhealthy-looking child, what is your mother feeding you, IF anything" in *babushka* (accompanied by an eye roll shared between me and my daughter when we discuss my mother's special vocabulary), and is always followed by a-not-so-subtle invitation to "*Priezzhai ozdorovit'sya k nam*," which means "Come and visit us to become healthier." I challenge you to both pronounce the above and to *not* feel like a terrible parent when this is said to your child.

RUSSIAN *BABUSHKAS* BUY THEIR GRANDCHILDREN ANYTHING THEY WANT

Obviously within reason, and that reason depends on (1) availability, (2) accessibility, and (3) levels of parental opposition. I grew up in the Soviet Union, otherwise known as the country with the highest per capita number of people who read books in the metro and the lowest per capita number of people who had access to consumer goods worth having access to. For my grandparents, this meant that to find a birthday gift for their one and only granddaughter, they had to come up with a collection of acrobatic moves worthy of the best Olympic gymnasts if those Olympics took place in the maze of the who-is-the-right-person-to-know-and-bribe economy. For example, (1) + (2) equaled a gold medal if you bought your granddaughter a newly released cassette player that no one else in her circle of friends had. On the bright side, they didn't have to deal with (3) until my father and I got into our next fight and he complained it was because they were spoiling me.

My parents now live in the consumerist heaven of the world, otherwise known as the United States of America, and they have neither the availability nor the accessibility problem. But, if you ask them, they'll tell you they've had the parental opposition problem, and that was because I was mean and didn't want my daughter to have every gadget her classmates had or a $200+ bag for her school books. In my mind I was engaging in parenting that was *not* a show-off competition with the other made-in-America-Russian-*babushkas* living in my parents' condo but, in their mind, I was an uncaring mother *and* daughter who was blocking them from showing off their granddaughter with her new Michael Kors bag full of Amazon- and Apple-produced devices.

RUSSIAN *BABUSHKAS* TAKE THEIR GRANDCHILDREN ON TRIPS TO FAR-FLUNG COUNTRIES

In my case that was to the Kremlin for the annual children's New Year's tree celebration, which for a Soviet kid was the hottest ticket in the country. They had the best candy and the best roundelay; but who am I kidding, the focus was on the candy. Every year I waited with bated breath as my grandparents tapped into every one of their *blat* connections to produce a coveted ticket to the event that fueled my sugar addiction and my snooty I-went-to-the-Kremlin conversations with friends for weeks. My grandparents also took me to a sanatorium on the Black Sea once, but I have no memories of this, except for the one where my grandmother and I agreed on a contest in which we competed for the title of the most prolific letter writer. In one activity, she got me to remember that my parents still existed while on vacation away from them, and practice my grammar, which was, hands down, the most success anyone's ever had with a young teen. Add to this that she made sure she let me win and you'll understand why I miss my *babushka*.

My daughter's trips weren't as enticing as the Kremlin ones, but my parents took her to France for a Côte d'Azur holiday, which is a phrase I haven't yet been able to utter in relation to my own life and I'm now past the mid-century mark.

RUSSIAN *BABUSHKAS* PREFER THEIR GRANDCHILDREN TO THEIR CHILDREN AND THEY AREN'T AFRAID TO SHOW IT

If your child has a Russian *babushka*, don't expect that *babushka* to spend the valuable moments she could be spending with her grandchild with you. It could be jarring at first, I'll admit, to have a baby and lose your status of being someone other than a feeding machine just as irreparably as your abdominals following a C-section, but this is the world we live in. You'll have to find peace with being ignored and relegated to the back burner and, take it from me, the best way to do it is to look for a silver lining. Mine was "at least as an only child I spent the first 30 years being the favorite child," and here's how I arrived at this.

Playing favorites was the natural order of things in the Soviet machine of competitive child-rearing. Kindergarten and school teachers had their favorite students; ice-skating and gymnastics coaches had their favorite athletes; Pioneer and Komsomol leaders had their favorite *apparatchiks*-in-training, so why couldn't parents have their favorite children? And while teachers and coaches based their favoritism on either your knowledge or skill or the ability to organize enough *mukulatura*[3] gatherers to win a competition (as was the case with my physics teacher who was also our homeroom teacher and really appreciated my activism while paying zero attention to my complete lack of knowledge of the subject), parents based their preferences on age.

Growing up I didn't want a sibling—it suited me perfectly well to be an only child. This was because living in the Soviet Union taught me that the important things in life, such as

- the kilo of mandarins my mother ripped out of the hands of that queue-cutting-excuse-of-a-Soviet-citizen after standing in line for hours

---

3 Paper recycling, also known as a potential death trap or pedophile paradise, because it involved young children going from door to door on their own in large tenements to ask people for their old newspapers. I'm still surprised I came out of this alive.

234

- the *Vesna* cassette player that my grandfather used his *blat* and a jar of red caviar from his World War II veteran's care package to procure
- the entire contents of my father's suitcase whenever he came back with new clothes from one of his trips to Poland or Yugoslavia

weren't meant to be shared. Neither were your parents' affections. And before you accuse me of being an egocentric narcissist who hogged both the mandarins and the hugs, let me furnish you with a couple of visuals of what it meant to have a sibling. Think of them as dioramas of Soviet family relationships based on the painstaking research I plan to never do.

If you have an older sibling—in the diorama that's the figure with the adolescent acne—be prepared for him/her to torment you on a regular basis (and always when your parents aren't home). If that sibling is a boy and has bicep power, he'll hoist you up onto the top of your parents' wardrobe while you scream in terror, developing what you'll later refer to as "a fear of heights brought on me by my idiot brother." If that sibling is a girl and has eyeliner power (a.k.a. the power of being old enough to own eyeliner), she'll make you drink three cups of tea without milk to earn the cup with milk you asked for *and* to earn the right to try that eyeliner. You're depicted in this diorama as a tiny figurine whose tears are larger than the teddy bear she's hugging, but clearly not large enough to compensate your older sibling for the misery they've endured since you were born.

If you have a younger sibling—and you're the asshole in all of the above—that misery is known as the "Why is [insert name of your younger sibling] always your favorite?" question you pose to your parents. You're depicted in this diorama as Harry Potter when he still lived under the staircase at his uncle's house, and your younger sibling is depicted as Dudley Dursley. Unfortunately, though, that's where the similarities end, because, unlike Harry, you won't become the most celebrated wizard in the history of wizards—or, as he was known in Soviet lore, Pavlik Morozov.[4] Instead, you'll spend your childhood getting yelled at for everything Dudley's done and you'll spend the rest of your life jealously eyeing the best cuts of duck on his plate. Gulag-style furniture in this diorama stands for the injustice you've had to endure by having to be born first.

If you have no siblings—you experience none of the above AND get an entire room all to yourself in a 345-square foot, two-room apartment. In this diorama, you're depicted wearing a new Yugoslav sweater, playing a bootlegged Bruce Springsteen tape on your new cassette player, and munching on your tenth mandarin.

Because obviously life seems better in the last diorama I never complained about being an only child. Instead, I thanked my lucky stars—or Lenin and the Politburo as they were known in the USSR—that my parents found the long, arduous road to communism too difficult to navigate with more than one offspring, and instead decided to bestow all their love, attention, and deficits on me. I had a good run of it too—until I had my daughter at 30 I

---

4 A Pioneer who betrayed his land-owning father to the Bolsheviks. Our Soviet history books told us he did it because he believed in the Revolutionary cause, but I think he must have been an older child and was just exacting revenge.

continued to be their favorite child. So, it was only fair to allow my mother the chance she missed out on when raising me. To her credit, she wasted no time in catching up, and soon had that whole dynamic of playing favorites down as if we were still living in the Moscow of mandarin and toilet paper shortages.

My daughter has been my mother's favorite child for the last 20 years and, okay, fine, I'll admit that it would have been nice to be noticed and maybe inquired about and perhaps even cooked for when visiting during that time. But, hey, there's always light at the end of that proverbial tunnel and mine is that my daughter is now a grown-up. Which means she has less time for her grandmother and since that time has to be filled with something, my mother has turned her attention back to me. She's already asked me about my life two-and-a-half times and that's only in the last three years. Things are definitely looking up for me.

RUSSIAN *BABUSHKAS* ARE OPINIONATED ON HOW YOU MUST PARENT

They consider themselves "hands-on" grandparents, which is also known as "not like those American grandmothers and grandfathers who see their grandchildren maybe once a year for holidays" and as "if you rely on me for help with your child, you should heed my opinions as if they were coming from God or, better still, from the mother who birthed and raised you." Here you'll recognize the influence of capitalism on the made-in-America-Russian-*babushkas*—they consider babysitting your child a favor, whereas the Russian *babushkas* of my childhood thought of it as their grandmotherly duty. I spent literally entire summers and almost every afternoon with my *babushka* Betya and I don't remember my parents ever parenting me according to her (much gentler) specifications.

In conclusion, I'm not sure if I'll end up becoming a Russian *babushka*. Time will have to tell—time and my daughter, who'll probably end up augmenting the list of Russian *babushka*'s traits I made above as soon as I make my debut as one. Because if she was able to zero in on that one characteristic of being a Russian grandmother when she was a toddler, she'll definitely recognize more of them as soon as any child of hers starts jumping on my couch.

LETTERS TO MY DAUGHTER OR THINGS ALMOST EVERY SOVIET-BORN PARENT WILL AT SOME POINT SAY TO THEIR AMERICAN-BORN CHILD

Well, aside from—(1) keep food out of your room when you visit; (2) remember to turn off the lights in the bathroom; (3) pick all those clothes up off the floor, please, and especially that shirt you borrowed from me and never returned; (4) dishes don't wash themselves; (4) I love you more than life itself, but my patience has very real limits; and (5) while away at college, calling your mother is good karma—there are a few other things I think my daughter should know to fully appreciate her upbringing, even if it came with an occasional cleaning-up requirement.

Dear Eliana,

Do you remember how you used to sneak into the kitchen at one or two o'clock in the morning because you were hungry and your young, growing body needed Oreos or SmartFood or a plate full of spaghetti? And how lots of times I told you this wasn't a good idea because your body was supposed to be resting and not digesting during the night, and that eating that deep into the HBO late night hours wasn't good for your health or your teeth or your mother's insomnia? And do you remember how I mentioned that I never ate at night at your age since having the munchies wasn't a Soviet thing, mainly because there were *no* munchies to be had in the refrigerator or in the pantry?

I kind of lied there a little bit. Not about the munchies, because that was true, but about me never eating at night.

When I was 12 I was hospitalized for about a month. There were eight girls in the room and we were all in for the long haul because the department in which we convalesced was some kind of "infectious diseases" department, although none of us appeared infectious. I was there with a recurrent sinus infection and maybe just having the word "infection" in your diagnosis was enough to bolt the doors and ban all visitors. Picture Covid times when you weren't allowed to accompany a loved one to a hospital, then populate that reality with a decrepit Soviet building where anyone could roam at will and, thus, possibly sneak onto a floor where "infectious" children were locked away "for their own good." Barricade that floor with an old door that locks with a key the size of your middle finger, then lock that door and give the key to a *babushka* who manned the Moscow anti-missile system during World War II and knows the meaning of the phrase "they won't pass." What you get then is a long queue of parents on one side of that door, and a long queue of their apparently infectious spawn on the other—all of them using their *borscht* receptacles to speak through *the same* keyhole for a meticulously-timed-by-everyone-three-minute-long conversation. What you don't get is any supplemental food packages.

I don't remember what they fed us in that hospital, but I remember I was hungry all the damn time. And because I spent my mornings being held down by nurses while the doctor drove a needle the size of his arm into my sinuses without anesthesia, and my afternoons trying to convince myself he hadn't scooped any of my brain cells as he cracked what felt like the entire insides of my scalp on his way up and sucked out the pus on the way down, my still-developing body needed calories to face the same procedure the next day. And so, every night, my roommates and I waited until all of the night nurses were on the other end of the long hallway either sleeping or drinking themselves into oblivion or watching the latest installment of *Sledstvie vedut znatoki*, a Soviet crime drama show. Once the coast was clear we made our way to the kitchen and binged on the stale, cold cream of wheat until our stomachs entered that dairy-induced bliss only Soviet breakfast cereal cooked with full-fat milk could induce, or until the neighboring room demanded their turn, whichever came first.

My last day of this life of midnight crime coincided with the adenoid surgery the doctors decided I needed. That morning, instead of my usual skull-cracking-sinus-pus-sucking procedure, the nurse brought me to an operating room and, in lieu of anesthesia, tied me to a chair. "It'll just be a second," the doctor said, and asked me to open my mouth. "I'm only going to measure first, I promise." The naive idiot that I was, I parted my lips thinking that when he really needs to go in and yank those adenoids out, I'll keep my mouth tightly shut. Then a grenade exploded inside my head and set fire to me, the doctor, the nurse, the building, and the stale cream of wheat I planned to plunder that evening. I screamed as loudly as the gurgling noise my throat was making would allow, because we needed a fire brigade and we needed it fast. "One down, one to go," the lying cheat of a doctor said, and at that point I couldn't really be strong and keep my charred lips together, so they pried my mouth open and exploded another grenade and then patted me on the back and said, "Good girl, you get ice-cream today."

Let me tell you, I loved ice-cream as much as the next tween who regularly scouted ice-cream kiosks in search of the elusive *plombir* that showed up for sale almost never. And, sure, in a Soviet hospital ice-cream was a fair deal for scooping the roof of my mouth free of its lining (see what I did there?). What wasn't fair, however, was that they were giving me only *two* scoops, they were giving them to me some THREE HOURS after unpeeling me from that satanic chair, and it was going to be *my only sustenance* for that day. Cream of wheat wasn't going to cut it for me on that midnight raid; this shit was getting serious.

That evening we crept slowly along the hallway the way we did every night and, sure enough, the cream of wheat was there—still in a huge pot and gelled over as usual. My roommates made a beeline for it, but I focused my attention on a few remaining loaves of bread, stale but still edible. I reached for one, ignoring a faint but annoyingly persistent voice of reason telling me that the stale bread might not be the best idea for the scorched earth my throat had become, when I noticed a pair of beady eyes staring right at me. A mouse sat on top of one of the loaves and regarded me with a "scoot away now, I was here first" kind of expression.

The scream that came out of my mouth a second later summoned all the nurses into the kitchen before my roommates could wipe the traces of the stolen cream of wheat from their mouths and night-gowns. The nurses punished us by getting the *babushka* with the keys to LOCK THE KITCHEN DOOR for that night and all of the following nights. Thankfully, while the commotion was going on all around me I had enough presence of mind to stow some of that stale bread under my nightgown. Then I hid it under my mattress and feasted on it for the next few nights in a Soviet, thank-you-comrade-Brezhnev-for-our-glorious-childhood-munchies kind of way.

Good thing you've grown up with the availability of real munchies. And of anesthesia.

Do you remember how every spring of your teenagedom I'd open the doors of your closet, pull out the drawers of your dressers, and reach deep under your bed, your desk, and the piano to extract all sorts of clothes you were calling "so last season"? How I'd ask you to take your eyes off Snapchat or Instagram or whatever other social media platform you'd disappeared into and tell me if an item of clothing I was holding was destined for the donation bin, the second-sale bin, or the bottom of the "just in case" shelf? And how at the end of this backbreaking work of hauling and folding and sorting I'd end up with at least two trash bags of clothes which you'd replace the very next day after a trip to Pull & Bear? And how you'd model them for me amidst the removed labels strewn on the floor and I'd look at you through the misty tears of everlasting love and impending dread of our next spring-cleaning?

Let me tell you—the words spring-cleaning weren't part of my lexicon until I moved to the US. In Moscow, we had nothing to donate or sell second-hand, let alone spring-clean out of our apartment of 345 square feet. My closet contained exactly six outfits,

MARGARITA GOKUN SILVER

which, by my last estimation of your wardrobe, is about 1/1,000,000
of yours. Those six outfits weren't all new—or even purchased. Some
were the adaptation of my mother's "last season" pieces, if by last
season we mean the pre-World War II era, and others were clothes
she and I had sewn using patterns we copied from the *BurdaModen*
magazine. This is how the process usually worked:

- A smuggled-in issue of German *BurdaModen* made the
  rounds at my mother's workplace.
- By the time her turn came, it was several-months-old, weath-
  ered at the edges, and sewn from so many times that I'd seen
  a few of its designs riding the metro.
- We copied the patterns we liked using old issues of *Izvestia*
  and *Pravda*.
- Then we scoured Moscow for fabrics.
- Then we spent several weeks sewing one outfit.
- Then I wore it until an irreparable hole sprung up in the
  subpar Ivanovo fabric not meant either for beautiful foreign
  replicas or heavy every-day Soviet use.
- Rinse and repeat with the next *BurdaModen* issue.

In other words, I'm glad you've grown up with Pull & Bear. And
that I don't have to remember how to thread the sewing machine
anymore. And that even though I always need a chiropractic adjust-
ment after hauling away those spring-cleaning bags, we get to spend
time together while throwing away your clothes, much in the same
way my mother and I spent time together while making mine.

Do you remember how at five you were cast to dance the part of a tiny fairy in *The Nutcracker* in one of those older-than-Gorbachev dance schools of St. Petersburg? How you, a tiny cherub-cheeked munchkin, had one of the starring roles in a ballet par excellence while I, along with the rest of the parents and the grandparents and the aunts and the uncles and the cousins of the performers, ohhh-ed and awww-ed in the audience as you pranced on stage next to the big girls and boys? And then, do you remember how during the rhythmic gymnastics practice you snaked your ribbon, or spun your hoop, or caught your ball while simultaneously sliding into a split every Soviet-born mother would shed enough proud tears for to replenish the Aral Sea? And how you jetted off to Atlanta or to Tampa or to some other American town your grandmother braved turbulence to take you to so you could compete at a meet? Do you remember coming home with a trophy and maybe a win and definitely a suitcase full of gifts you deserved for contorting your body the way neither God nor evolution ever intended? And, then, do you remember I told you a story about how, when I was young, I also performed a routine worthy of the Bolshoi stage while simultaneously tossing my bright red ribbon into the air to celebrate the coming of the communist paradise?

About that last one. Never happened actually.

My ballet—and, by extension, any possibility of the adjacent rhythmic gymnastics—career ended on the first day it began, and namely when my mother brought me to a local Palace of Pioneers to sign me up for an after-school ballet activity. The matron in charge took one look at me—and by "one look" I mean a continuous stare that slid down from my still somewhat chubby neck to the thighs she was pursing her lips at—and said, "She's too fat for ballet." Granted, I was no Maya Plisetskaya, and if you've already read the *I Feel Bad about the Back of My Head* essay, you'll know my legs were as far removed from the ideal of a Russian ballet beauty as kindness was from the Soviet ballet industry; but, at seven years old, I didn't yet know that. Still, if people were good at anything in the Soviet Union—aside from, well, aside from being good at ballet and gymnastics and other disciplines that involved a thin frame and straight legs—it would be at telling you straight up that you'd be crap in all of those. Which I suppose I should have been thankful for, because I was never ever going to make it in the world of Russian ballet and would have probably bled to death from my toes while needlessly trying.

All of this is to say that I'm thrilled you got to dance, and to throw that ribbon, and to even seriously entertain the idea of becoming a "doctor-ballerina" one day.

Do you remember how you came home from school one day and told me that a classmate had asked you where you kept your striped pajamas? And how you recounted that he had also told you to "go to the gas chambers" and that others in your class WhatsApp group routinely texted "Hail Hitler"? And how I was horrified that history was repeating itself and not in an abstract or Nate Silver kind of way, but in a very personal "how is it possible that my daughter is on the receiving end of the same insults as I had been 30 years earlier and WTF and how is this happening in a supposedly advanced and democratic Western society" kind of way? I think I might have offered to go and yell at everyone at your school, to which you very wisely—and may I add, in a totally poised, confident, and badass kind of way—replied, "No need, mother, I got it." And do you remember how that made me so proud and so teary that I lost it right there and then and hugged you for all of eternity and then some?

I was *not* like you, kid. I confronted antisemites exactly zero times, instead pouring all my efforts into the ostrich-inspired strategy of "if they don't see me, they won't know/remember/realize I'm Jewish." Sadly, that only occasionally worked, and *only if* my Soviet passport and my birth certificate and all official roll call documents where our ethnicities were recorded with more attention than ever went into Chernobyl's design were MIA. What worked eventually was packing up and immigrating somewhere I thought neither my offspring nor I would ever have to turn in our shoulders and hang our heads because we belonged to one of the 12 tribes.

It didn't quite work the way I imagined. Because nothing ever working the way you imagine is one of the glitches in the world's operating system. Another glitch is that antisemitism is still a thing, and without being an actual clairvoyant I can tell you it's here to stay. Because for humanity to let go of its oldest hatred we'd all have to become better people and lose all of our prejudices, which is way more difficult than agreeing that Hitler was a horrible person, but some people apparently still take issue with that. So, I'm glad you're using your voice and speaking up against the same evil I was too much of a chicken to take on. And that even though this is one instance where your coming of age and my coming of age seem to coincide, your response to it is as different as our respective reactions to the mess in your room.

Lots of love,
Mama

PS: You forgot to turn off the light in the hallway.

GREAT EXPECTATIONS,
THE WRAP-UP (KIND OF)

Very appropriately, I'm writing this essay on the 31st of December.[1] Appropriately, because wrap-ups are fashionable at year ends but also because New Year's Eve is the biggest holiday in Russia and among the Russian diaspora. And since this year—aside from gifting us yet another evidence of humanity's general ineptitude to band together in the face of a crisis—also marked 30 years since I emigrated, I thought it might be a good mid-point to evaluate the state of my Russianness. Which, you'll remember from the first essay in this collection, I set out to eliminate completely after I landed in the US and changed my name. And so now, as I take a look at my years as an immigrant and also at my pantry which, on this day, contains one of the largest tubs of mayonnaise Costco's ever sold, I'm here to come clean and admit that I didn't quite succeed. My Russianness has persisted—possibly in the same way Putin's presence continues to hover over what remains of Trump. Or over what remains of the GOP and #MoscowMitch. Or, Politburo-save-us, over our future elections, our democracy, and our computer systems.

But there's hope! (For me—I'm not sure about our elections or our democracy.) That hope, everyone knows, comes from light, and so in the best teaching traditions of philosophers whose names I

---

1 Of 2020, if you must know. The year you only add to your age because you have to and also because this is the year Trump finally lost for real.

don't remember and also of Leonard Cohen, I'm going to illuminate some of those Russian habits I still apparently harbor. I'll peer deep inside myself—as deep as those Kremlin hackers are probably now peering inside my Mac—to decide (1) what I'm going to keep and (2) what I definitely don't want and still need to work on to repress like it's 1937. Here's an almost complete list—almost because life is always a work in progress and also because the title of this essay says "The Wrap Up (Kind Of)."

1) WHAT I'M KEEPING

THE NEW YEAR'S EVE CELEBRATION

Here's how we celebrated New Year's Eve in the Soviet Union:

- Prepare in advance by procuring (via *blat*) all the difficult-to-find food items like smoked sturgeon, caviar, and cured sausages.
- On December 31st, spend the entire day making dinner for that night: make all of the *zakuski* I mentioned in the *Water with Dinner? Pour Me Another Glass* essay, plus make a main course, plus make a cake for dessert.
- Stock up on vodka and cognac.
- Seriously, stock up on vodka and cognac.
- Wrap gifts up in old issues of *Pravda* and *Izvestia* you haven't yet used as toilet paper and place said gifts under your New Year's tree.

- Gather together as a family and sit down for dinner around 10 p.m. to say farewell to the old year.

- If you're a grandfather, dress up as Ded Moroz, the Russian Santa with a much better fashion sense and enough income to afford a human assistant, a.k.a. Snegurochka, the Snowmaiden, to ring the doorbell and deliver gifts to your grandchildren (make sure your slippers don't show under your long, elaborate robe, because kids are observant).

- Open *Sovetskoe Shampanskoe*, the Soviet Champagne (sorry, France and PDO laws) at several minutes to midnight.

- Toast each other as the Kremlin clock strikes midnight and express hope that next year will be better than the one you've just drowned in kilos of mayonnaise and liters of vodka.

- If your neighbor doesn't have keys to the roof of your building or if that neighbor is already indisposed from too much vodka, tune into the main channel to listen to Brezhnev/Andropov/Chernenko/Gorbachev make a speech promising that next year will be better than the one you've just drowned in kilos of mayonnaise and liters of vodka.

- If your neighbor has the keys to the roof of your building and is still sober enough to lead you there, make it to the roof and try not to slide off its icy surface as you watch the fireworks.

- Have dessert and watch *Goluboi Ogonek*, the Soviet version of *The Dick Clark Show*, until you succumb to either vodka or mayonnaise-induced stupor.

- Next morning, eat the *zakuski* leftovers for breakfast.

Here's how—according to our limited immigrant knowledge—most Americans celebrated New Year's Eve:

- If you're young, don't mind the cold, and live anywhere near a large city, make your way into that large city and try not to be crushed by the crowds as you lose your voice screaming in excitement.
- Go back to a friend's house, get drunk, and maybe eat some cold, leftover pizza.
- All other cases—have something to eat, maybe stay up until midnight, have some bubbly if you did, and go to bed no later than 12.30 a.m.

Which one of those rituals sounds more fun? Even if it involves complicated, queue-heavy, *blat*-dependent preparations? Right. My point exactly.

It didn't matter how much I wanted to assimilate or become a fully fledged American, their New Year's celebrations never felt enough. Which is why—after a few years of celebrating it like an American—I decided to infuse my New Year's Eve with a few Russian elements. I started small, which basically meant watching *S Legkim Parom*[2] and

---

2 Perhaps your 1970's Soviet equivalent to *Love Actually* but really a Soviet romcom that (1) was enough of a tear-jerker to fool Soviet censors into overlooking its biting satire; (2) is yet more proof that everything good in the West—romcoms included—was invented in the USSR.

mandating gift exchange,[3] but a few years ago I went even further and started making *Olivi'e*. Which, if you ask anyone born between 1918 and today in the largest country on Earth by landmass, is dedication. It's also the Russianest thing to do on New Year's Eve. So, if anyone were giving out marks for assimilation, I'd get a D here, but, when it comes to celebrating New Year's, it's totally worth it.

TEA WITH SWEETS

Honestly, I don't understand how you can drink tea without anything sweet. And I don't mean sugar or honey or Stevia but honest-to-goodness death-by-carbohydrates-something next to your cup. Sure, that whole unsweetened-herbal-tea-at-bedtime ritual is probably good for your health, but nothing is as good for your spirit as a fully caffeinated cup of the darkest brew served with either a piece of cake, or a cookie, or some chocolate, or, if none of those is available, a few spoons of jam in a small bowl—just like nature and your childhood nostalgia intended. (Grade for assimilation among Americans—again a D, but worth every calorie.)

BLINI ONCE A WEEK (AT LEAST)

I love carbohydrates. I love them in all shapes and sizes but I especially love them when they are pancakes. And when they're served

---

3 I cannot emphasize this enough. You can have birthdays, you can have Valentine's Day, you can even have Hanukkah, but gifts on those days will never be as important as New Year's gifts.

for breakfast with something sweet to put on top and accompanied by black tea (we've discussed that above). So, after I discovered—on our arrival in the US—that pancakes came in a box and required a total 1/100,000 of the prep time they needed in Moscow, I was like, "Yes, sign me up and fill my pantry with those boxes."

Until I tried them and they tasted nothing like the pancakes of my childhood. I mean, don't get me wrong, they tasted like some kind of dense-with-a-definite-trace-of-not-quite-natural-ingredients pancakes and, if you'd never had grandmother-made-from-scratch pancakes, they might have sufficed. But I was spoiled by that home-made taste and aroma that only Soviet flour and eggs could produce, and so I cleared out my pantry and attempted to make my own *olad'i*.[4] About 5,396 times.

They NEVER rose. Which, if you know anything about the art of Soviet cooking, is a felony and not a misdemeanor. Sure, they tasted fine and could have probably passed for the pancakes I devoured as a child, but ONLY IF I closed my eyes and ignored their lack of fluffiness as resolutely as I tried to ignore my culinary failures. But flat pancakes are flat and that makes them not pancakes at all. It makes them *blini*, the Russian equivalent of crepes (although don't tell a French person that),[5] which is how I arrived at the carbohydrate concoction I could make, be proud of, and call "my most favorite breakfast," even if that got me another D in the assimilation course.

(I'm done with food, I think. Probably not done with the Ds.)

---

4 Russian for pancakes and mine for an "unattainable childhood memory."

5 And, on second thoughts, don't tell a Russian person that either.

ACCENT

I've tried for years, really, to eliminate all traces of foreignness from my English speech, but native speakers still hear it because at some point in the conversation they always get a quizzical look on their faces. Like they're trying to solve a puzzle, or guess the answer to a complicated riddle, or figure out what their next chess move would be against Kasparov. Then most of them venture out to ask, and here's how that conversation usually goes:

A NATIVE ENGLISH SPEAKER: You have a bit of an accent, but I can't place it. Where are you from?

ME: Russia.

A NATIVE ENGLISH SPEAKER: Oh, really?

ME [nodding]

A NATIVE ENGLISH SPEAKER: Your accent doesn't sound Russian at all.

For my first 20 years as an immigrant I loved hearing this because I didn't want to sound like the worst villain in the history of villains, a.k.a. the person with the "scariest accent ever" as defined by Trevor Noah. From 2016 on I loved hearing it because I didn't want to sound like a troll who engineered Trump, and like that troll's employer who put him in the White House. Now I love hearing it because I feel like I'm doing my part in dispelling the myth that all Russian speakers sound alike. And that their accent is the least sexy accent on Earth and maybe even in the galaxy.

I've made peace with keeping that odd, unrecognizable accent, precisely because it's unrecognizable. Also, speaking with an accent but not *speeekeeen viz a khevi RRRRRussian aksent* should get me some points for assimilation, or at least for harboring lower levels of Russianness, right? I think I get a C+ here, at least. (The + is for some presence of sexiness.)

FASHION

I dress up to walk my dog Pushkin. Not high-heels-full-make-up kind of dressing up but there's-no-way-you'd-ever-catch-me-anywhere-in-public-in-a-pair-of-sweats-or-active-wear-unless-it's-in-a-yoga-class kind of dressing up. My husband doesn't understand this, so a typical conversation in our house sounds something like this:

MY (AMERICAN) HUSBAND: Why do you always have to dress up?

ME [in front of the mirror trying to ascertain if the pair of jeans I'm planning to wear goes well with the sweater I picked out]: I'm *not* dressing up—I'm wearing jeans [moving on to choose a necklace to go with the sweater].

MY (AMERICAN) HUSBAND [pointing to the necklace]: And this?

ME [picking out shoes to complement the ensemble]: What?

MY (AMERICAN) HUSBAND [shaking his head and heading out the door in a pair of sweats]: We're going to walk by the beach.

ME [selecting a scarf]: And to lunch! [Taking another half an hour to decide on a purse]

Yes, I know I get another D for assimilation, but who cares when that scarf goes so well with those shoes.

2) WHAT I'VE BEEN WORKING TO DISCARD

ENVY

Let me tell you, it's not easy to get rid of envy. Especially if you grew up and came of age in a country where all consumer goods worth having were available never and envy was one of the most prevalent emotions, second perhaps only to fear. In the Soviet Union people envied each other for:

- Clothes, if they came from anywhere outside the USSR.
- Shoes, if they came from anywhere outside the USSR.
- Furniture, if it came from anywhere outside the USSR and if buying it involved *blat*.
- Electric equipment, including, but not limited to, washing machines, vacuum cleaners, and sewing machines, because buying those always involved *blat*.
- Cassette players, because you couldn't get one if you didn't have *blat*.
- Cars, if you didn't have a car.
- Zhiguli, Model 5 or Volga, if you had a car but a different (read: worse) kind.
- Personal toiletries, if they came from anywhere outside the USSR.
- Make-up, if it came from anywhere outside the USSR.
- Shampoo.
- Real toilet paper.

The list could go on and on, but I'm going to wrap it up by saying *everything* could potentially be on that envy list. The rules were pretty simple—if you didn't have something, you envied someone for having that something.

When we arrived in the US, envy got a makeover. Sure, some consumer goods were still on the list—designer-anything, a German-made car (or, even better, two of them), a beachside penthouse condo in the Porsche building—and could still make you a target of your fellow émigré's green monster. But more than the actual things you could buy, it was the stuff that allowed you to buy those things that now topped the list. Namely, money. And a job that made you lots of money. And education that allowed you to get the job that made you lots of money. And schools that allowed you to get the education that got you the job that made you lots of money. And pre-schools that… Anyway, you get the idea. Envy flourished and replaced fear as a Soviet émigré's prevalent emotion (unless it was the fear of socialism and Democrats who, as every former Soviet Trumper knows, are the same exact thing).

It kind of makes sense. I mean, if you come from a country where everyone went to the same state schools, got the same state university education, and then got the same jobs with pretty much the same salaries, envy doesn't go further than consumer goods and maybe an occasional vacation. Especially since you could go months without seeing someone in a jacket they'd bought off some scalper who dealt in Yugoslav imports. But in America the possibilities were endless and communists weren't there to subvert them. And because we all bought that "pull yourself up by your bootstraps" ideology with as much gusto as we shopped for our first pair of Levi's, we figured envy would just drive us to succeed. Which brings me to my next discard.

DISAPPOINTMENT

Do you know when I realized that the state of my Russianness was still strong? After my daughter brought home her first B. And my first, second, third, and hundredth reaction was that of disappointment and of how dare she fail her family in such a spectacular manner? The same reaction appeared when she quit piano lessons, didn't get the absolute maximum on her International Baccalaureate, and didn't get into Harvard (or even apply there). Basically, whenever she did anything that didn't qualify her for a Nobel Prize I felt the same exact disappointment my parents usually directed at me. Known as "nothing you ever do is good enough" and "even if you got an A+ you should have gotten it with distinction" and "Sveta's mother told me she got all A+++++" and "she also got first place in that ice-skating competition, *takaya molodetz*,"[6] this is a sentiment that is to Russian-born parenting what *Olivi'e* is to a Russian-celebrated NYE. And it also brings me to my next discard.

CRITICISM AND CONSTANT COMPARISONS WITH OTHERS WHO ARE ALWAYS DOING BETTER THAN YOU ARE

Comparison is the parent of both envy and disappointment. "Unfavorable comparison to others is the mother of all success"

---

6 Means "she's so impressive" in Russian and "why aren't you like her?" in Soviet parent.

was a slogan inscribed on the brains of most Soviet parents, and right under Lenin's name on the front of the mausoleum. When paired with the critical comments our parents have wielded far better than the FSB nerve agent team have ever covered their tracks, it made for a Novichok-strength cocktail that chipped away at your self-esteem much like the real Novichok could wreck your insides.

JUDGING AND SNOBBERY

My mother's favorite question as it applied to my friends or the girls I hung out with at school as a budding teen was always this: "*U nee est' sterzhen'?*" Which is pretty much untranslatable into regular English—the direct translation would be "Does she have a rod?" which you'll admit sounds borderline obscene and definitely *not* what she had in mind. What she did mean, though, was the following:

- Does this girl smoke?
- Does she get drunk at parties?
- Does she have regular sex?
- Does she dress "slutty"? (Her word, not mine.)
- Does she have an "easy" reputation? (Again, her word—not mine.)

Having a *sterzhen'* meant NOT doing any of the above and instead being a model Komsomol member en route to a *doska pocheta*, a politicized Soviet equivalent of an American honor roll. I lied whenever she asked me that, not only because I didn't want her to interfere in my friendships, but also because I didn't want to be judged on the basis of who I chose to befriend. And while judging girls—and only girls—by what they did, how they looked, and who their friends were may not have been limited to the Soviet Union, overachieving is a thing among Russian-born, so, naturally, we took it much further. We've expanded it to everyone else.

Obviously, I can't speak for everyone, but pretty much 99.9999999 percent of Soviet émigrés are judgmental and snobby. Never has a saying been as descriptive of a group of people as "*Vstrechayut po odezhke*"—"We'll form our first impression of you by what you wear"—has been of former Soviets. It's basically a euphemism for "We'll decide your value and character by what you look like, and by that we mean (1) your clothes, jewelry, and accessories; (2) whether you have any tattoos or piercings; (3) if you behave in a way we don't approve of (see bullet points above, yes they still apply); (4) what kind of car you drive; (5) what kind of dog or cat you own and if it has been shipped from the best breeder in Europe; (6) your background, and by that we mean if you have a good education, if you come from a respectable family and if your family has a good education, and whether there are any luminaries in your family and if so, how important and rich they are; and (7) if you own a piano."

The second section of that saying is "*Provozhauyt po umu*," which means "Our next impression of you will be based on how smart you are"; but, because in the US the knowledge of Gödel's Incompleteness theorem is a lot less important than the model of the car you drive, it's been replaced with "*Provozhauyt po* how many apartments you have in NY and in Miami and whether you fly first class or take your own yacht to Europe each year." Once it's been determined that your standing on the totem pole of successful humanity is lower than their own, snobbery kicks into that barely visible but very much felt glance in their eyes, flick of their eyelashes, and smile that's as laced with condescension as Putin's enemies' underwear is laced with nerve agents. If you need any evidence of snobbery being a driving cultural force, look up the Russian-language magazine named *Snob*. Yes, there is actually a magazine with that name and IT SELLS.

MAYONNAISE

I almost never eat mayonnaise anymore but I'm including it here because *Olivi'e*, sadly, is two-thirds mayonnaise.

I'm not proud to admit it, but some of the things I mentioned in the second section still occasionally rear their archaic heads. But the good news, I think, is that I notice it when they do. Because, you know, vigilance is key. The US wasn't vigilant and remember what happened in 2016? And then, of course, acting on that vigilance is key too. So as soon as I sense any of the above stirring up shit inside me like the best of Putin's Twitter trolls, I try to crush them with the same zeal Trump's campaign courted those trolls. But I don't always succeed, unfortunately. Just ask my daughter. Wait until after New Year's, though. Because she's also busy making *Olivi'e* and tonight we'll have a three-way WhatsApp with her and my mom and compare our respective creations.

It might have taken me 30 years, a lot of soul wrangling, and even more anguish-induced stomach cramps, but I've realized I didn't need to become a completely assimilated American to be different from the girl who left Moscow in 1989. All I needed was some of that American freedom I believed would help me explore who I wanted to be, the determination to let go of those Iron Curtain scraps that didn't serve me, and the perseverance to both ignore and banish the critics. Once I got the hang of that, keeping bits and pieces of Russianness (and sometimes even passing them on!) suddenly didn't seem so bad—even if they involved mayonnaise.

A LETTER FROM MARGARITA

If you're reading this note, hooray—you got my book and are now proficient in all sorts of Russian swear words as well as privy to the bombshell secret Putin's been hiding from the rest of the world.[1] On those two accounts, I hope I haven't disappointed, and that you have enjoyed this quirky account of one girl's journey towards near-perfect fluency in English and all things USA. If you have loved this book even a little bit and want to keep up with the latest news from me and my publisher, you can sign up here:

www.thread-books.com/sign-up

(Your email will never be shared, and you can unsubscribe at any time.)

If I tell you I wrote this book because these stories just begged to come out, it wouldn't be an exaggeration. Although there've been other memoirs of Jews emigrating from the Soviet Union to the US and elsewhere, I have yet to find one told from a female perspective. And while I'd never claim to be the Amy Schumer or Jenny Lawson or Samantha Irby of my Soviet-Jewish-girl generation, I hope you've found parts of these essays funny, even if the events they describe

---

1 My editor wants me to qualify that it's not really a bombshell but an open secret, but I'll let you judge for yourself.

aren't usually considered to be fodder for humor and even though I wrote this in the midst of the Covid pandemic and as I cared for a loved one with cancer.

Thank you so much for reading this book, for going on this journey with me, and for occasionally (or maybe more than occasionally) laughing out loud. Reviews are the writer's candy and so if you enjoyed *I Named My Dog Pushkin*, please leave one. You can also send real candy and/or connect with me either via my website or Twitter.

I'd love to hear from you (unless you're employed by a certain Russian troll factory) and please don't tell Putin who spilled his secret!

Margarita Gokun Silver

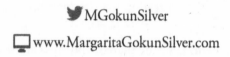

MGokunSilver

www.MargaritaGokunSilver.com

ACKNOWLEDGMENTS

To show how seriously I take these acknowledgments I'll set the scene for you: I'm writing this wearing the outfit you've read about in one of the essays—the top/skirt ensemble I'd bought specifically for the red carpet. I've got an impressive library of important books behind me, an open Zoom window in the iPad in front of me, and a nice bottle of bubbly next to me. Because this is as red carpet as it gets during Covid but also because I haven't actually been invited onto a red carpet (yet).

Therefore, I'd like to start by thanking those execs who will read this book, see great potential for a series—on HBO, Netflix, Hulu, or whatever other streaming service will get invented between the time I write these words and the publication of the book—and get the series made starring Claire Foy as me. (Not because she played the Queen in *The Crown* but because she and I look like twins—go ahead, Google it.) I also want to thank those of you who, over the years, listened to my immigration stories, told me to write them down, and promised to buy the book if it ever came out. I'm thrilled you've kept your promises.

Thank you to everyone who has ever read anything I've written and to those of you who supported me while I worked on this book. Huge gratitude goes to Nicola Prentis—her emotional support and eagle-eyed notes made my (often shitty) early drafts worth editing and completing. Additional thanks go to the many writers I know with whom I've commiserated on how this thing we call "a writing career" could often make you giddy and miserable—all in the space of one hour.

To those in charge of aligning the stars—kudos for the job well done. This book came at a time when humor seemed inaccessible and yet its writing kept me sane during the long days of both the umpteenth Covid lockdown and caring for a loved one with a cancer diagnosis. Those of you who might wonder how in the world I did it, I have two words for you—well, actually two statements: (1) if you spent a decade wanting to see these stories out in the world, you take that chance whenever it comes; and (2) *nadezhda umiraet poslednei*, which you'll remember means "hope is the last to die" in Russian.

Thank you to the team at Thread and, especially, Nina Winters for seeing this book's potential at its very early stages and for helping me shape it into a manuscript that Pushkin himself (the poet, not the dog) would probably consider a fun read. Nina's detailed notes as to which lines made her laugh out loud went a long way to lessen my crippling self-doubt, a condition that only a great champion and a fantastic editor can assuage.

Thank you to the friends who fielded my numerous WhatsApps and phone calls during this turbulent time of perfecting my sentences while waiting for a doctor's phone call on my husband's test results. My unending gratitude goes to Elaine Chisholm, Antonella Lo Re, Elli Zisis (the best yoga teacher in the whole of Greece), and Yael Cobano. To *The Great British Bake Off* and Netflix I owe a giant debt of gratitude for ensuring that my evenings were much sweeter than my days.

ACKNOWLEDGMENTS

And finally, to my family—this book wouldn't have happened without you. Mainly because I wouldn't have had enough to write about, but also because your support during these uneasy months has been invaluable. Thank you to my parents for all of your help, love, and (occasional) understanding. Thank you to my husband for keeping positive through all the mayhem; no humor or writing would have been possible without your hope for a good outcome. And thank you to my daughter for being my everything, for allowing me to write about you, and for never failing to remind me that motherhood has been the best adventure of my life (even if it included a sporadic "Russian mother" reference).

To Pushkin (the dog, not the poet), your cuddles are the best even if you're always reluctant to give them.